Gondwana Theology

Garry Worete Deverell

Gondwana Theology

A trawloolway man reflects on Christian Faith

Garry Worete Deverell

ATF PRESS

Adelaide

2024

First published by Morning Star Press in 2018.
Front cover painting: Glenn Loughrey
Cover design: John Healy (for the design).

This edition 2024 by ATF Press

ISBN:
978-1-923206-40-3 Softcover
978-1-923206-41-0 Hardcover
978-1-923206-42-7 Epub
978-1-923206-43-4 PDF

SCAN ME

Published by:

Making a lasting impact
An imprint of the ATF Press Publishing Group
owned by ATF (Australia) Ltd.
PO Box 234
Brompton, SA 5007
Australia
ABN 90 116 359 963
www.atfpress.com

Table of Contents

Acknowledgments and Dedication

This book could not have been completed without the help of a great many friends and colleagues. Dorothy Lee talked my reluctant self into taking to the field over many months. Celia Kemp and Mark Brett read the manuscript in detail and made many helpful coaching suggestions. Lil Deverell, Naomi Wolfe, Victor Joseph and Glenn Loughrey cheered from the bench. Chris McLeod kindly agreed to pen a forward. Trinity College Theological School and the Bishop Perry Institute provided an invaluable writing grant across two years. My home parish of St Stephen and St Mary, Mt Waverley, through its vicar Dianne Sharrock, granted the study leave I needed to complete the manuscript. Mary Schramm, Jodie Deverell, and Shane Matthews lent me their homes and their hospitality when I was able to get away to write. Amanda McKenna did a great editing job on my manuscript. I am grateful to these and many other colleagues for their faith in me, especially when I didn't have much faith in myself.

I am particularly grateful to Uncle Glenn Loughrey for gifting his painting 'Treaty' to grace the cover of the book. A gift I can never repay except with my thanks.

I dedicate this book to my daughters Erin and Gretel, with a prayer that they may find in their heritage a deep well from which to draw in good times and in bad.

Foreword

Following the end of World War 2, theologians could no longer do their task as if nothing had taken place. They were confronted with a world greatly changed; only a theology written in the shadows of the horrors of Auschwitz was possible. Only a theology that confronted the truth about the capabilities of humankind for good and evil was going to speak with any real integrity. Reconciliation between people, nations deeply estranged, and the creation of a new world of peace, was dependent upon the acceptance of the truth of the events that shattered the world; and the God of hope who enables the truth to be told.

There have been some real attempts at reconciliation within Australia between Aboriginal and Non-Aboriginal Australians, yet the wide gulf between the two still needs to be bridged. There are some who will say that I exaggerate, and surely things are not as bad as I say. To those I would say that Garry Deverell's book highlights that the truth of the colonial destruction of the Aboriginal way of life, together with the post-colonial traumas that beset many contemporary Aboriginal Australians, still needs to be told, and, even more importantly, accepted. Denial is never too far away for those who want to gloss over another's hurts, and downplay the harm committed. There are many in Australia who do just that. Truth telling, however, is painful business. The Prophet Isaiah saw this clearly when he heard people of his time saying, 'do not prophecy to us what is right; speak to us smooth things . . .' (Isa 30:10).

A post-colonial theology in Australia is only possible if we are able to face up to the past events that so traumatised generations of Aboriginal Australians and accept that much of it was executed by the hands of our non-Aboriginal forbears (I too, like Garry, am a product of two worlds, and share in the history of both perpetrator and victim). In accepting this, we will also see that much suffering continues in the lives of Aboriginal Australians as successive waves of government, and everyday Australians, ignore our voices.

Garry's book is an important foundational text in the continued writing of a post-colonial Australian theology. Much of Australian theology has perpetuated the nation's own mythology—mateship, a fair go, ocker egalitarianism, a land with abundant wealth and 'boundless plains to share.' If these were ever true, a quick look at our nation's newspapers, television commentators, and social media, let alone the official pronouncements of government, show these myths are dying very quickly. Theology in Australia needs to be placed on a much surer and truthful footing.

Garry's book is a work of integrity and truth as he reflects on his own experiences of ministering in a church that has not always been able to hear the voices of Aboriginal Australians. He brings clarity and insight to the theological task, locating his own, and others', experiences of being Aboriginal as a way forward for the theological task ahead of us. I thank Garry for this obvious labour of love, and I commend his work to those who wish to develop a theology for a contemporary Australia that steers the course between nationalistic myth building, and importing theology created elsewhere for other peoples, in other places. This book is a work of theology grounded in truth and giving rise to hope.

The Right Reverend Chris McLeod
National Aboriginal Bishop
Anglican Church of Australia

Chapter 1
First Peoples Spirituality

Defining spirituality

The word 'spirituality' is a much-contested term. In Australian discussions, it most often refers to a special kind of personal or private experience by which the 'spirit' within engages with a 'mystical' and otherworldly realm of pure spirit. I would prefer to use the word in a more Jewish and Aboriginal sense: spirituality as an entirely ordinary, irreducibly earthy, way of life that is nevertheless informed and enabled by the Spirit of God.

Consider the creation stories we find at the very beginning of the Hebrew Scriptures. 'In the beginning, when God created the heavens and the earth . . . the Spirit of God was hovering over the waters' (Gen 1:1-2). In Hebrew, the word for spirit, *ruach*, can also be translated as 'wind' or 'breath'. When God creates the world as we know it, with all its ecological diversity and brilliance, it is the spirit or breath of God who presides over it all. Note, however, that the work of the Spirit of God is not to create beings of pure spirit or mind, as some contemporary spiritualists would have it. It is to create a material cosmos made of flesh and blood and earth and stardust. What God creates is all that we have come to know as an order of ordinary fleshly existence: flora and fauna, sun and moon and stars, land and sea, women and men. Indeed, the Genesis account of the creation of human beings emphasises our earthliness. The first human being is named 'Adam', a play on '*adamah*', the word for 'dirt' in Hebrew (Gen 2:7). Adam is made from the stuff of earth in the same sense as trees are the stuff of earth: both are born from the ground (*cf* Gen 2:9). But what makes the earthly flesh of Adam alive? It is the breath or Spirit of God breathed into his nostrils (Gen 2:8). So, for the Jewish mind at least, 'spirituality' can never be cordoned off from ordinary, fleshly existence. It is not a special experience or heightened awareness of that which is somehow beyond this plane. Spirituality is entirely about this world. It is about living this life in the knowledge that God has made and loved us as we are, in all our fleshly materiality, and that God sustains us in that life through the animating gift of the Spirit, who is like the very breath in our nostrils.

The First Peoples of Australia are just as unlikely as Jews to locate spirituality in rare or special experiences or claims about privileged knowledge concerning the supernatural or otherworldly. For us, spirituality is all about the most basic building blocks of life: country, kin, and the practise of a ritual storytelling that weaves past, present and future living together in a web sometimes referred to as 'the dreaming'. Let's say a little about each in turn.

Country

The fundamental basis of every Indigenous way of life is our relationship with the land of our ancestors. The first thing one Aboriginal or Torres Strait Islander will ask another when they meet for the first time is 'where is your country? Where is your sea?' For the particular country or body of water from which we come represents not only a place of origin or of dwelling. It represents, also, a place of sacred communion with our ancestors, a communion in which we might learn both who we are and what our unique vocation or responsibility in the world might be.

My country is the far north-eastern region of Tasmania, a large island in Australia's south which my people often call trouwerner or lutruwita. I come from a mob variously known as the trawloolway or pairebeenenner. It is a beautiful country that includes the open grasslands around the Ringarooma river, the seaside port of leenerrerter (Bridport), the sheltered fishing lagoons of tebrikunna (Cape Portland and Musselroe Bay), wukalina (Mt William), larapuna (The Bay of Fires), and our sacred mountain poonerluttener (Mt Cameron), where the various family groups within our mob would meet to do business. Before the arrival of Europeans, my mob lived on this land for somewhere between 30 to 40 thousand years. Imagine that! We were here many millennia before the Egyptians build their pyramids and the Babylonians their gardens. We were here before the last great ice-age set in.

One of our creation stories tells how Moinee, a wombat-ancestor, took some earth up to the sky and used it to fashion Parlevar, the first trouwernen, who looked like a man but who had a tail like a kangaroo and legs without knee-joints. This meant that Parlevar could not lie down to sleep and was in great discomfort. Luckily, the star-ancestor, Dromerdeener, took pity on Parlevar by removing his tail and creating knee-joints. This made life far more comfortable for Parlevar! Parlevar lived in the sky with Moinee and Dromerdeener for a very long time, but eventually he decided to come to the earth by walking down the lore-way we know as the Milky Way. Moinee eventually followed and, in order to protect Parlevar, fought against many evil spirits, including the terrifying Wrageowrapper. Moinee also set about moulding the land so that it would provide sustenance and a pleasant habitation for Parlevar. In this he was helped by two other creator-ancestors. Laller, the ant-ancestor, cut the paths that would become creeks and rivers. Tarner, the kangaroo-ancestor, made great big dents in the ground which would became lakes. When Moinee's many other children fell to the earth in the form of rain, they also set about shaping the land. When their work in the landscape was finished, they lay down to form mountains, and small islands around the coast of trouwerner. Moinee himself became a large rock at kribbiggerrer (Cox Bight) in the far south of trouwerner. Thus the presence of our ancestors remains in the landscape, and in the many animals and plants they brought into being.[1]

The creation stories of Indigenous peoples show that country is more than just a dwelling-place for human beings. It is also the place in which the creator-ancestors live and continue to speak and guide through river, mountain, sea, and myriad animals and plants. The land is therefore something of a sacred text for Indigenous peoples. Properly read and understood, it shows us who we are and what we are to do in this world. Jews have their Torah, and Christians their New Testament, but Aboriginal and Torres Strait Islander peoples have our land and sea. By attending to its secrets, the call and address of the divine can be clearly discerned.

1. As told by Woorraddy, an elder of the nuenonne people of Bruny Island, and Manalargenna, my ancestor from the trawloolway people of the North-East, to George Augustus Robertson. See NJB Plomley, *Friendly Mission: The Tasmanian Journals and Papers of George Augustus Robinson, 1829–1834*, 2nd edition (Hobart: Quintus Publications, 2008), 368, 373, 376.

Kin

A second marker of Indigenous spirituality is kin. When an Aboriginal or Torres Strait Islander person meets another, the second question they ask of each other is 'Who are your mob?' When I am asked this question, I reply 'I belong to the trawloolway pairebeenener mob in trouwerner (Tasmania)'. You may know a little of the history of our mob after the Europeans arrived. It has been recounted at great length by historians such as Lyndall Ryan, Henry Reynolds, Aunty Patsy Cameron and Nick Clements.[2] At first relations between ourselves and the newcomers were cautiously polite. But then, as settlers granted themselves increasingly large tracts of rich river country stretching into the interior of the state, their farming animals and activities threatened both our food supplies and our sovereignty, so we began to spear sheep and cattle in order to supplement our food stocks and dissuade the settlers from pushing even further into our lands. The response from Europeans was brutal. Vigilantes were formed to go 'native hunting'. Whole families and groups of families were massacred in settler raids which then gave rise to what is called (by white historians) the 'Black War', which raged all over Tasmania during the late 1820s. Amongst the fiercest of our warriors during this period was the last head man of our trawloolway mob, Mannalargenna. I am his direct descendant. The combined effect of war and European disease decimated our numbers. From an initial population of perhaps 18,000 palawa (people) there were now only a few hundred of us left. A man named George Augustus Robinson, an Anglican lay preacher, was appointed the 'Protector of Aborigines' and set about roaming the island looking for survivors. He promised that if we put down our weapons and came in from the bush we would be granted a large portion of trouwerner on which we might live and prosper beyond the law and weapons of the invader. He knowingly lied. In fact, the majority of us were taken to a camp on Flinders Island where many of us perished from a lethal mix of grief

2. Lyndall Ryan, *Tasmania Aborigines: a history since 1803*, (Sydney: Allen & Unwin, 2012); Henry Reynolds, *Fate of a Free People: a radical re-examination of the Tasmanian wars* (Melbourne: Penguin, 2004); Patsy Cameron, *Grease and Ochre: the blending of two cultures at the colonial sea frontier*, (Sydney: Angus and Robertson, 2011); Nick Clements, *The Black War: Fear, Sex and Resistance in Tasmania*, (Brisbane: University of Queensland Press, 2014).

and European disease. When the group had dwindled to less than 50, we were transferred to a camp at Oyster Cove, south of the main settlement in Hobart.

Most of the 23,000 people who identify as Aboriginal palawa (people) of Tasmania today trace our ancestry to the peoples of the North-East mob, my mob. Even before the 'Black War' had erupted, many of our women were kidnapped by lawless sealers who plied their trade in and around the shallow waters surrounding the Bass Strait islands. One such man was Mr George Briggs who, at some point in the early 1810s, procured my ancestor Woretemoeteryenner—a daughter of Mannalargenna—as his domestic partner. As far as we can tell, this was a marriage of convenience rather than love. Aboriginal women were initially abducted by the sealers in order to satiate their sexual hungers. But over time, the women proved themselves to the sealers as masters of both sea and bush craft. Some of the woman, at least, were possibly given in marriage by their clans in order to buy some kind of uneasy détente with the sealers. Briggs named his first child with Woretemoeteryenner 'Dalrymple' Briggs. She was born in 1812, probably at Port Dalrymple near the mouth of the Tamar River. Through a sequence of events that remains unclear, their daughter was removed from her mother and adopted by a European couple in the emerging township of Launceston. In 1814 she was baptised Dalrymple Mountgarret Briggs and taken into the legal guardianship of Dr and Mrs Mountgarret. 'Dolly', as she was now known, continued to have access to her birth mother and saw her regularly when she came to the settlement with her husband to trade seal skins. This access ceased when Woretemoeteryenner was taken by Robinson to his newly established prison camp on Flinders Island in 1830. There she remained for the next ten years, until Dolly—now married and living with an ex-convict near Perth—petitioned the colonial government to release her into Dolly's care. As the prison camp was being wound down at around that time, Dolly's request was granted. So Woretemoeteryenner came to live with her daughter in 1841 and reportedly delighted in assisting with the care of Dolly's eight children. Shortly after the family made a move to the district of Dunorlan in 1846, Woretemoeteryenner fell ill and started to construct her own funeral pyre. She died a few days later. Dolly and her husband, Thomas Johnson, eventually produced 11 children and settled in the Latrobe area of North-West Tasmania. Through their daughter Charlotte, I am part of their mob.

So, when Aboriginal people talk about kin, they certainly mean it in the usual sense of biological family. But there is a second meaning of kin, for us, and it is deeply connected with our spirituality of land. Because we believe that our country is still filled with the presence of the ancestor-creators who formed it a long time ago, we also regard all that is alive in that land as our kin, our family. For we are descendants of those ancestor-creators. We are their offspring. That is why, whenever we approach a new place that is not familiar to us, we talk to the spiritual presences in the land, the ancestor-creators, asking for their permission to cross that country and for their protection while we are there. For, unlike the children of modernity, we do not take the country and its resources for granted. If we take from the land for our survival, if we harvest its resources for our nourishment, we ask permission and we give thanks to the ancestor-creators for their bountiful provision. We are also careful to take only what we need, for to do otherwise is to endanger not only our own survival, but also the continued existence of our ancestor-creators, who continue to live in and from the land as much as the land lives in and from them.

Most Aboriginal and Torres Strait Islander mobs give special honour to a particular ancestor-creator that is associated with a particular animal. For some of the mobs in the top end, it is the tortoise or the Dugong. For others, those of us who live inland, it is the turtle, the platypus, the crow or the wombat. For my own mob, because Moinee made us from dirt and modelled us on the kangaroo-creator Tarner, it is the Forester Kangaroo that is so plentiful in the Tasmanian bush. For us, Tarner is kin. Traditionally we were dependent on Tarner for most of our protein, and so we fire-farmed wide open grasslands in order to provide them with a pleasant place to live. The traditional hunting of kangaroo was therefore done with great respect and ceremony. We gave thanks to Tarner for being willing to offer his life, over and over again, for our sustenance and survival. We hunted only what we needed, and nothing was wasted. His furs became our winter coverings. Her fat was mixed with ochre to make ceremonial paint, but it was also used to make our woven water containers watertight. His guts were used to make bags and ropes.

'Dreaming'

We have now come to our final marker of Indigenous spirituality, that ritual weaving together of land, lore, and kin—in each of their past, present and future dimensions—that is often referred to as 'The Dreaming'. The dreaming is sometimes mistaken for a series of mythological stories describing events from long ago. In this rendering, the time of the dreaming is past and has no direct bearing on the present or the future; it is also mistakenly assumed that the dreaming is something akin to a Platonic 'Idea': that it exists nowhere as an actual body or material reality, but only as the shadow of a chimera in the collective memory or longing of a people. In fact, nothing could be further from the truth! For the dreaming is not primarily about the past. It is like the presence of Yahweh in the burning bush encountered by Moses on Mt Horeb (Exodus 3): it is everywhere and always present, in the living things all around and like the breath in our own nostrils; it is a past rendered meaningful, a future full of promise, and a present aflame with life in all its fulness.[3] The dreaming is nothing less, in fact, that the passage of the divine Spirit in and through the world as body, materiality, lore, flesh.

Being such an all-encompassing reality First Peoples—as with every other people—can often forget that the dreaming is real. Like fish swimming in water, we can often forget how crucial the water is to our survival. It is all about, providing food and a pleasant habitation; it also fills our lungs with the oxygen that keeps us alive and alert. Yet, so often, we cannot see the water as anything other than the substance through which must navigate to get what we need. In this sense, the water often becomes invisible to us, nothing more than a dimly perceived transparency in and between the more solid objects of our desire and affection. What renders the dreaming visible to our lazy, amnesiac awareness, is storytelling. And not just any storytelling. *Ritual* storytelling: story told, enacted and performed in the body.

Those creation stories we talked about earlier were not, traditionally, communicated and retained through the print-media I am using in this booklet. They were danced in communities as vivid and sensate renderings of traditional knowledge or lore. As children grew into adulthood, they were taken to particularly sacred places, places of power in which the landscape itself sung aloud its secrets, and there taught the stories in the form of ritual dances and songs. Here, in a

3. My understanding of the significance of Exodus 3 is deeply formed by my reading of Richard Kearney, *The God Who May Be: A Hermeneutics of Religion* (Bloomington & Indianapolis, Indiana University Press, 2001), 25–31.

carefully designed liturgy, the ancestral stories were inscribed on the bodies of our children as part of their growth into adult membership of the tribe. For what they learned in these rituals was who they were and how they were to live in harmonious community with both country and kin. Knowledge of any kind is, as every primary school teacher knows, much easier to remember if you learn it kinaesthetically using repeated patterns of sound and movement. When the sound and movement also tell stories—big stories about the cosmos, the environment, and our place within it—then the patterns form a ritual narrative by which traditional knowledge is passed on and maintained. This passing on of a body of knowledge—sometimes called the 'lore'—from elders to new initiates, is precisely the process which colonisers sought to disrupt. For they knew that the very survival of Aboriginal and Torres Strait Islander peoples *as* Aboriginal and Torres Strait Islander peoples depended on it. That is why they removed us from country, separated us from our elders, and forbade us to speak or sing or otherwise perform our language and lore. They wanted to remove us from our dreaming and kill our spirit. But that is easier said than done! For while the connection of our people to our dreaming can indeed be damaged and disrupted, it is almost impossible to extinguish altogether. For the dreaming itself continues to call to us, even in the most dire circumstances imaginable. Even when the traditional rituals have been forgotten and the songlines by which we navigated the continent survive only in fragments, the landscape itself speaks to us.

Here I want to share a personal story. As a young man at University for the first time, I would often go bushwalking with my new friends. On one occasion we went for a walk through pydairrerme country on what is now called Tasman Peninsula, trekking our way through the dense forest to Fortescue Bay. As is often the case when walking with a group on a well-maintained but narrow track, the line spread out, the fittest and most silent moving quickly ahead and the slow talkative ones falling behind. As we finally neared the first curvatures of the bay, I found myself quite alone. The voices of my companions were barely discernible in the distance behind me. As I came toward the beach, I heard another group of voices, sometimes singing, sometimes chanting. I must confess that my first thought was 'How did these tourists find this place!?' But I quickly realised that the voices were not speaking in English, or Chinese, or any tongue I could remember, but in a deeply musical language which immediately impressed itself upon me as both far more ancient and far more melded with the landscape in which I found myself. It was as though the very trees and rocks and birds were speaking to me in this strange but sonorous tone. I followed the voices until finally, emerging from the treeline onto a beach, I saw a large gathering of people. Their skin was black. They wore the hides of native animals and red-and-white patterns of ceremonial ochre covered their faces, arms and legs. They were dancing around a fire, now crouching, now standing tall, hands rapidly moving from front to rear to head, in clear and unmistakable imitation of cockatoo, kangaroo, snake. As I appeared at the edge of the beach, I suddenly realised I could understand their song. Which was really, really, odd, because most of my people's language was—especially at that time—lost. I knew only a few words. That these *were* my people was immediately clear to me. But they were not my *contemporary* people. They were my ancestors. The old people. The voices and forms of the dreaming itself. For a moment they turned to face me. They recognised my presence by a smile, a nod of the head and a raised hand of greeting. But then I heard my walking companions drawing closer, their voices becoming both louder and more proximate. I turned my head in their direction, eyes wide with wonder, and then back to the scene on the beach. But now it was not there. It had vanished. Only the voices of the wind and the birds, and the tide as it caressed the sand, remained. 'What's up' asked one of my companions, 'You look like you've seen a ghost.' I didn't know what to say.

I share this story to demonstrate two important truths. First, the dreaming cannot be confined to the past. It is about the present and the future as well. It is happening all around us, if we have the ears to hear and the eyes to see. Second, the dreaming can break into the experience of even the most colonised of Aboriginal people, as the people of trouwerner surely are. At the time when I had this waking dream (if that is what you would prefer to call it) I was a very young man who knew about and valued my Aboriginal ancestry but had really just begun to explore what it meant. Today I believe the ancestors wanted to encourage me on that pilgrimage of exploration. They wanted to reach out to me in the midst of the landscape my mob had inhabited for millennia. They wanted to confirm me in the baby steps I had begun to take towards more fully embracing who I was as a trawoolway person. Their gamble paid off. I saw, I heard, I stepped out in faith.

Chapter 2
Towards a Theology of First Peoples Spirituality

Some may wonder at why I've called this chapter 'A Theology of First Peoples Spirituality' rather than 'A First Peoples Theology'. I do so because I am a post-invasion Christian who is seeking to understand my Aboriginal heritage in the light of Christian theology, rather than a pre-invasion Indigene who is seeking to understand Christian faith in the light of supposedly pre-colonial understandings of cosmos and of dreaming. By describing myself in this way, I am simply acknowledging that colonisation has happened and that there is nothing that anyone can now do to wind the clock back toward some kind of pristine, pre-contact, Indigenous imagination. Obviously, many of my people are engaged in recovery projects of many kinds: recovering language, recovering history, recovering lore, recovering songlines, recovering spirituality, and so on. These are worthy projects that have my full support and from which I draw liberally to enhance my personal sense of what it means to be palawa and trawloolway. But I take it as incontestable that all such projects nevertheless utilise post-invasion imaginations and methods in order to accomplish their ends. Our Indigeneity is, in other words, a colonial Indigeneity. It is an Indigeneity that is forever entwined, both for good and for ill, with the fact of colonialism, with its imagination and its performative effects in hearts, minds, economies and culture. To pretend that we can somehow return to pure forms of pre-contact Indigeneity is nothing less than a platonic fantasy.

What is true at that macro-level is also true of the micro-domain of theology. For a First Nations person even to *use* the term 'theology' is to acknowledge that she or he is looking at their spiritual experience and commitments through a lens that includes all that the European versions of Judaism and Christianity brought to this country. For 'theology' is an Indo-European word and an Indo-European discipline. Of course, all over the world theologians from non-European backgrounds are rightly seeking to transform theology so that it draws more deeply from extra-European wells of imagination and method. I am, myself, one of those theologians. While this trend is to be welcomed and applauded, it is nevertheless true that the discipline of theology will never escape its European roots or imagination. Nor should it! For theology has always been an inter-ethnic work of translation and reinterpretation. European thinkers, many of them as indigenous as it is possible to be within the migratory patterns of European history, brought the discipline of theology into being by engaging texts and rituals from the ancient Near-East; and they did so in synagogues and churches that were founded by missionaries from the ancient Near-East. As they engaged this 'foreign' data, they sought to repeat and render the faith there contained in a form, and with an accent, that was palatable to European hearts and minds. They wanted their faith to be in continuity with the faith of the Near-East sages, but nevertheless different: readable, liveable, habitable by a people from their own lands, cultures and languages.

It was, of course, always already thus with the sharing of the 'gospel' proclaimed by the Jewish-Christian apostles. The canon of the New Testament itself speaks of the gospel's intrinsic impulse towards cross-cultural iterability. Although Jesus spoke a form of Aramaic, most of the New Testament is written in Greek, the *lingua-franca* of the Roman empire in the first century BCE. Furthermore, it is clear from the writings of both St Paul and the Evangelists that they understood their gospel as a re-rendering, a re-understanding, of the whole history of Jewish faith, particularly in its prophetic and messianic dimensions. Nor were they shy when it came to transforming their message yet again as it crossed over from Jewish to Hellenistic communities. The language changed, certainly, and with it many nuances pertaining to cosmology and culture. But so, also, did many of the moral and ethical practices they required of their converts. In the minds of the apostles, this was not only possible, but necessary. For their God was one who created and loved all people, from every nation and ethnic group, a God who wished to address them within the fleshly materiality of their own distinct languages, landscapes, and cultural practices. For God's word had come to them finally and uniquely not as an immutable 'Idea', forever pure and unchangeable in the heavens, but as a person who spoke a particular language and followed particular traditions; in short, the word of God had come to them as Jesus the Nazarene. In Jesus they learned that the word of God's continual and persistent *gravitas* was to become flesh, materiality, landscape, culture. He also confirmed in them the Jewish insight that the word of God is forever a pilgrim or a traveller in the world. Jesus, it seems, was forever on the move, crossing social, religious and ethnic boundaries in order to proclaim the good news of God's grace to everyone he met on the way.

His death and resurrection made possible, it seems, an even more expansive radicalisation of these themes. For now the Spirit who animated Jesus' ministry in Palestine, the Spirit forever imprinted with Jesus' character and face, was released into a missionary church. The Spirit inhabited the first Jewish Christians and imbued them with the impulse to roam still further in their pilgrim ways. That is how the good news came to reproduce itself otherwise in myriad voices, cultures, rituals and cosmologies the world over. Even, in these latter days, unto the First Peoples of Australia.

The gospel and colonisation

The movement of Christ's gospel into the Indigenous communities of this country was, and is, far from straight-forwardly positive, however. There is a saying in Aboriginal and Torres Strait Islander communities: 'When the white man came, he made an exchange: the bible for the land and the sea'. Actually it was far worse than that in most places. It was the bible in exchange for our languages, lore and kin as well. As has now been documented at great length and in much detail, the removal of our people from the sources of our sustaining spirituality had a crushing effect on our health and well-being. The loss and trauma suffered by the first generations who encountered the invader is still, it seems, in effect. For Aboriginal and Torres Strait Islanders remain the poorest, sickest, and in every way the most disadvantaged members of contemporary Australian society.

Doing theology under the crushing weight of this legacy, whether by apparently European or apparently First Nations people, is therefore far from easy. For there are hazards in every direction. The most common form of theology in this country continues to exercise a strategic forgetting about the genocidal sin at the foundation of the nation. It proceeds as though the doctrines of discovery and *terra nulius* were still firmly in place and therefore no one was dispossessed of their land or sacred texts, no one was illegally or immorally massacred, no one was removed from his or her family in order to destroy their way of life. The vast majority of theological utterances I have heard and read from apparently 'Australian' theologians continue to pretend that none of this has happened, that the vocation of Australian theology need be nothing other than a positively framed elaboration on steadfastly European concerns and themes. Obviously, I object to this stratagem in the strongest possible terms. For Australian theologians to ignore the cataclysm that befell, and continues to befall, this country's First Peoples as a direct result of European invasion is like European theology failing to engage with the great genocides of that continent's bloody history, the horrors of the Nazi persecution of Jews most prominent amongst them. A theology that fails to engage and reckon with the worst that human beings can do to one another is no theology at all. For theology is, in its deepest marrow, a search for the truth about God, the universe and ourselves. And if it is not about the truth, it more properly belongs to the genres of romance or fancy. Much Australian theology is therefore, in my assessment, a *fantasia* built upon lies, obfuscations, a sequestering away of the truth. Such theology is of no help whatsoever in realizing the reign of God on earth. If anything, it colludes in the colonial project and is therefore a foundation contributor to the Australian sin of forgetting.[1]

1. There are a few notable exceptions, that all tell a very similar story to mine. See Anne Pattel-Gray and John P Brown, *Indigenous Australia: A Dialogue About The Word Becoming Flesh in Aboriginal Churches* (Geneva: WCC, 1997); Mark G Brett, *Decolonising God: The Bible in the Tides of Empire* (Sheffield: Phoenix Press, 2009); Jione Havea & Mark G Brett (editors), *Colonial Contexts and Postcolonial Theologies: Storyweaving in the Asia-Pacific* (Basingstoke, UK: Palgrave MacMillan, 2014); Jione Havea, *Indigenous Australia and the Unfinished Business of Theology: Cross-Cultural Engagement* (Basingstoke, UK: Palgrave MacMillan, 2014); Chris Budden, *Following Jesus in Invaded Space: Doing Theology on Aboriginal Land* (Eugene: Wipf & Stock, 2009); Noel Loos, *White Christ Black Cross: the emergence of a Black church* (Canberra: Aboriginal Studies Press, 2007); Peter Lewis, *Acting in Solidarity? The Church's Journey with the Indigenous Peoples of Australia* (Melbourne: Uniting Academic Press, 2010).

Though the greatest hazard for Australian theologians is also the most regularly practised, there are certainly other ways to dishonour the gospel of reconciliation. Also prominent is a strategy which, on the one hand, wants to tell the truth about what has happened to First Peoples in this country—activating a *mea culpa* and a call for lament and/or confession—yet also, and at the very same time, manifesting a complete disinclination to afford Aboriginal and Torres Islander people any kind of agency in designing a reconciled future that is habitable for all of us. A quick survey (via the web) of the number of Aboriginal or Torres Strait Islanders who enjoy a permanent seat in the senior councils of the Australian churches, or in their theological colleges, reveals that having a voice where it matters is still a very, very, very rare thing. At the same time, despite many fine words of repentance and apology, the churches continue to remain largely unconscious of the fact that the sins of the past continue to have their present effects, for which the churches certainly bear considerable responsibility.

The grace made known in Jesus Christ is not as cheap as this. Grace is not the name for a ghostly, disembodied, bloodless transaction that happens apart from our bodies, hearts and communities. In the New Testament, grace is the name given to a transformation of the relationship between human beings and God, certainly, but most especially human beings in their relations with each other. God takes the initiative in Jesus Christ, and in the costliest mode imaginable: a *kenosis* (self-emptying) of Christ's divine status, a torture and crucifixion at the hands of the colonial powers of his day. But grace does not reach its terminus, its intended goal, unless it surges through the bodies and communities for which Christ laid down his life. Unless those communities receive God's grace into themselves via a trans-valuation of all their previous values—a mirroring, responding *kenosis* with regard to the moral high-ground we might have chosen to occupy with regard to our neighbours—then grace has not yet become entirely flesh. Unless we put aside our pride entirely and welcome the crucified Jesus in the form and face of our crucified kinspeople, then grace remains nothing more than a platonic 'Idea', hanging splendid and beautiful in the heavens, but never real enough to change or transform people in either space or time. In a very real sense, the resurrection of Jesus into the glory of God will not be complete until the whole earth, including all those who have suffered injustice and discrimination at the hands of others, are also included in his bloody, costly, grace.[2]

A theology that seeks to engage both the grace of God made known in Jesus and the spirituality of First Peoples must therefore actually listen to our experience and take it seriously as data for theological reflection. Theology must treat our agency, our subjectivity as children of God with whom the Spirit has been walking and talking for millennia, as importantly as it treats the agency of the people of God recorded in the Hebrew and Christian Scriptures. It must, in other words, regard our experience with God, especially as that experience is embodied in our relationship with the 'dreaming', as a legitimate source of revelation.

The dreaming as Aboriginal and Torres Strait Islander scripture

In the first chapter, I wrote about the 'dreaming' of Aboriginal and Torres Strait Islander people as our encounter with the divine Spirit in and through the land, the sea, and all the abundance of living things that dwell therein. While Jews, Christians and Muslims have their written scriptures, I wrote, Indigenous people regard the land itself as a religious text. For it speaks, constantly, of our relationship with the divine, with the non-human biosphere, and with each other as human beings. But how are we to understand, from a European-Christian point of view, the role of the creator-ancestors who formed our sea and landscapes? Are they idols, even demons, as so many of the missionaries apparently believed? Could they not, more positively, be compared with the Angels by whom Yahweh sends his word and his will into human experience? Perhaps so. For my own part, I should like to propose that the creator-ancestors might be understood as roughly analogous to the figure of Wisdom celebrated by *Proverbs* 1:20-33 and by the *Book of Wisdom* as a whole:

> She is the breath of the power of God:
> pure emanation of the power of the Almighty;
> Nothing impure can find a home in her:
> She is a reflection of the eternal light,

2. I acknowledge, here, the remarkable theological work of Dietrich Bonhoeffer, especially in *The Cost of Discipleship* (New York: Touchstone, 1995).

> untarnished mirror of God's active power,
> image of God's goodness.
> Although alone, she can do all:
> herself unchanging, she makes all things new.
> In each generation she passes into holy souls,
> making them friends of God and prophets,
> for God loves the one who lives with Wisdom.
> She is indeed more splendid than the sun,
> she outshines all the constellations;
> compared with light she takes first place,
> for light must yield to night,
> but over Wisdom evil can never triumph:
> for she deploys her strength in all the world,
> ordering all things for good.
>
> (Wis 7:25-8.1)

Wisdom, in this tradition, is seen as a personal extension of God's creative light and power, a personality at once both distinguishable from God and yet sharing the very life of God with any soul who is open to her influence for good. For First Peoples, the creator-ancestors are like this too. While not exactly God in the Jewish and Christian sense—the one creator of all that is, seen and unseen—the ancestors nevertheless share in the creative work of God. They are charged with certain responsibilities in the creative process and, in their human-divine-animal hybridity, are ancient prototypes of the close relationship between human beings and the non-human world. They remind us of that relationship and call us to be careful that the relationship is honoured and maintained through an ongoing responsibility to care for country and keep the lore.

There are other analogues between the Judeo-Christian story and our Indigenous dreaming. In Jewish tradition, God made covenant with Abraham, Isaac and with Jacob, and took their semitic language and wandering pilgrim ways to God's heart. Through Moses, the covenant was confirmed and written down as law. In the sign of the burning bush, God chose to be God only with God's people, never apart from God's people. God chose to journey through the world in a way that was permanently joined to the fortunes, apprehensions, languages and practices of a particular people. God chose to be a God who, in a certain sense, could be owned and claimed and called upon, just as God continues to call upon all people to choose life rather than death, the good of God rather than evil, the land of promise rather than the wilderness of sin. My own people also remember various lore-givers, like Abraham or Moses, who led the tribes into new lands and gave them the basic building blocks for living the good life. In these figures we, too, gained a sense that the creator was our companion and our help, the promise of a good and blessed future, if we would only walk humbly in the ways set out for us.

In Jewish tradition, Israel abandoned the ways of God and was exiled to a foreign country, amongst a people who spoke a different language and worshipped different gods and had a different sense of what was good and just. Whilst there, Israel learned this language and this way. Some elements of this foreign way were ultimately judged to be good and helpful. These were incorporated into Jewish storytelling, law and theology. Some elements of Babylonian and Assyrian culture were judged unhelpful or even evil. These elements were either opposed or were transformed via careful exploration into more positive features. In a similar manner, my own people have many stories of individuals or whole clans being sent away from home and community because of wrong-doing. In those foreign places, demons and monsters were encountered. Demons who sometimes turned out to be great ancestor-spirits who had a teaching to share which, upon the return of the exiles to their communities, became sources of wisdom to help the tribe survive. We also believe that while the arrival of Europeans in this country two to three hundred years ago was evil, catastrophic and destructive on the most enormous scale imaginable, that it is nevertheless true that some of what the invaders brought counts as wisdom. The story of Christ, for example, through whom we learned of a God who suffers with and for the creation in order that this same creation might be transfigured, remade, in the image of the creator: that is a good story for a suffering people such as ours.

Some Indigenous theologians, especially from North America, have proposed that Indigenous mythology and ritual might be regarded as another 'Testament' in relation to the Christian faith received from Europe.[3] I regard the dreaming of my own people

3. See, for example, Clara Sue Kidwell, Homer Noley and George E Tinker, *A Native American Theology* (Maryknoll, NY: Orbis, 2001); James Treat (ed), *Native and Christian: Indigenous Voices on Religious Identity in the United States and Canada* (Abingdon, Oxfordshire: Routledge, 1996).

as analogically related to the deposit of faith brought from Europe, even if I remain critical of some of the latter's institutional clothing. The Christian tradition to which many First and subsequent peoples belong, whatever our ethnic inheritance, bears witness to a creator who ultimately, in the sign of the paschal mystery of Christ with us, welcomes all people—including all our diverse languages, practices and ethical sensibilities—to God's heart for ever. My sense as an Aboriginal Christian is that the rituals and stories which represent my own dreaming tradition have been embraced by God in the person of Christ just as much as those of the Europeans. For Christ, I believe, translates all tongues and cultures into the speech of heaven, which is a common speech at once older and newer than any language currently spoken. In this connection, I resonate with Emmanuel Levinas' distinction between the 'saying' and the 'said'. The speech and rituals of human beings, in all their variety and richness, are a 'said', a speech made for largely utilitarian purposes: for communication, for naming concrete subjects and objects, for negotiating our many wills and desires with others in the human project known as community. Yet such speech has both its origin and ultimate fulfilment in a 'saying' that, at once, both transcends and animates utilitarian speech from within.[4] The 'saying' is the language of the *eschaton*, the speech of a God who is always in motion, a dynamism at the heart of all human speech that is also the home and dwelling-place of all human *logoi* as it unfolds within the *sophia* of God. For God has chosen, it seems, to journey toward God's own future in and through the history of human beings, with whom God has made an unconditional covenant.

All of which is to claim that the God made known in the stories of the Jewish and Christian Scriptures is a God who was sojourning with our people, here is this country, long before the calling of Abraham, or Moses, or St Paul. Our dreaming can be 'read' as a legitimate witness to that sojourning and should therefore be engaged as an equally rich source of revelation and guidance regarding the living of a human life that is good, beautiful and true (*cf* Phil 4:8). In practise, that means that I feel entirely free to call upon both my Christian inheritances—Aboriginal and European—in the ongoing call to bear witness to the

4. See, for example, Emmanuel Lévinas, *Otherwise Than Being or, Beyond Essence*, translated by Alphonso Lingis (Dordrecht: Kluwer Academic Publishers, 1991), 5–7.

God who was in Jesus Christ. For that God is also in our dreaming and is certainly abroad in every time and place by the Spirit who indwelt and animates both.

Towards a First Peoples approach to the language of worship

Since most of my theological scholarship has been in the area of ritual and worship, it seems apt that I close this short reflection with some comments about creating a genuinely Indigenous liturgy for the Christian church in this country.

Aboriginal and Torres Strait Islander cultures are obviously very ancient. For much of our history, we did not speak with Europe, either its imagination or its rituals. But I must firmly resist the idea that First Peoples today are not also colonised peoples in our imagination and our practices. Aboriginal and Torres Strait Islander people today—certainly because we have been thoroughly colonised, but also because we have creatively adapted and modified the colonising cultures for our own purposes and ends—are deeply competent practitioners of what might be called an 'Australian' way of being that is neither monolithically imported nor indigenously Gondwanan.[5] And this is as true for the more 'traditional' and 'dark' peoples of the north as it is for the 70% of us who belong to the south of Gondwana and are apparently less 'dark' and less 'traditional'.

Aboriginal tradition, like any living tradition, has kept itself alive by adapting and integrating new events, languages, people and cultural practices, even those which were initially experienced as traumatic and life-denying. We have been doing this with our friends and neighbours (both human and terrestrial) for millennia. We have been doing it with European Christianity for over 200 years, and we will continue to do it with all people of good will as we seek to worship the God made known both in our dreaming and in Jesus Christ. The point I am making is that other people don't have to do it for us. They don't have to 'translate' some notion of European ritual into something that is, somehow, pure Gondwanan. Like everyone

5. I use the term 'Gondwana' in order to evoke a sense of the Australian continent as an ancient habitation for being, far more ancient than the settler histories of 'Australia' are interested to remember. The term was coined by Eduard Suess and derived from Sanskrit for 'forest of the Gonds', an Indigenous people now located in India.

in the human family, we are competently adapting our traditions to new circumstances, new insights, new eschatological dawnings. If you want to stand alongside First Peoples, or partner with us as we do so, that is great. But please don't assume that you have to do it either for us or in spite of us. We are like the Irish who, even when their language was largely forgotten and everyone had adopted the language of the invader as the *lingua franca*, nevertheless produced the poetic voices of Hopkins, Yeats, Joyce and Heaney who were able to transform the language that had transformed them in a peculiarly Irish way, so that English in Ireland could never more be considered the possession of the English alone.

What I would say to the denominational liturgical commissions is this: please, please, please let us help you produce a liturgy that looks and sounds like it comes from *this* country and not another! For, on the evidence of what I have seen so far, our liturgical commissions have barely begun to tap the wealth of a First Peoples spirituality of land, water and sky in order to reanimate our liturgy with a spirit of place, the Spirit of this place. Our official missals and prayer books are great yawning deserts, and not in a good sense. But let's be clear about why this is so. It is not because we lack liturgical writers, artists and curators—both First Peoples and settlers—who have all the spiritual acumen, theological insight and creative skill required to produce such rites. Many of us have been producing exactly the kind of thing that is required for over three or four decades now. The problem is not that the gifts have not been given. It is because liturgical commissions and bishops and denominational authorities are afraid of these gifts and simply will not allow our work to find its way into official books and offices and large diocesan rites.

What I am calling for is a kind of liturgical 'creole' that seeks to speak the language of Europe but in a First Nations way that clearly belongs to Gondwana. Where I am coming from, theologically, is the covenantal mystery at the heart of the incarnation. For a Christian view of the cosmos is necessarily covenantal. As I have said already, God chooses to come to Godself—that is, to God's identity and future—through the vulnerability of enfleshment, a fundamental marking and transformation performed and enacted through an unconditional commitment to humankind and to the cosmos. What the paschal passage of Christ through his world then reveals is not that 'God' and 'human beings' (as single-in-themselves identities) learn to talk with each other in a third space which might be called the ritual storytelling of 'liturgy' or, more broadly, 'gospel tradition', but that God is always-already human and humans are always-already divinely capable in their ritual speech.

The implications of this peculiarly christological anthropology are several. First, neither the gospel nor specific human languages or cultural practices are ever single-in-themselves entities in search of a conversation with each other. Rather, they are always already modes of such conversation. The gospel is always already a translation of a translation of a translation of the eternal word uttered by the Father in Jesus Christ and animating the hearts, imaginations and cultural performances of human beings in every time and place. Second, liturgical storytelling is not, therefore, an expression of the dialogue between a single-in-itself gospel and a single-in-itself local culture, but rather the eternal covenant or treaty between God and human beings. It is not an *expression* of the covenant; liturgical storytelling *is* the covenant in all of its dynamic trinitarian relationality and eschatological reserve. Third, the notion that there is a pure kind of liturgy that has to then be 'enculturated' as some kind of second step is therefore a redundant idea, in that the gospel covenant is forever a translation of a translation of a translation of the Christological mystery. It is not a pre-existing entity that has to enculturated. It can only *be* itself by virtue of cultural performance, that is, by bodily and sensate utterance in a communal setting. If we cannot hear or see or smell the gospel, it is not because the gospel is not being faithfully enculturated, but because we have simply deactivated both our senses and our imaginations in order to protect ourselves from its prophetic call. For the gospel speaks and cries aloud concerning death and life, cross and resurrection, baptism and eucharist, in all things: every bush, every body, every face, every utterance, every movement of fire, water or air, every disaster, every hope. The gospel therefore cries aloud in the rituals of the dreaming as much as in the rituals of Europe.[6]

---

6. Here I'm drawing on Louis-Marie Chauvet's post-structuralist critique of traditional Thomist categories in the masterful *Symbol and Sacrament: a Sacramental Reinterpretation of Christian Existence*, translated by Patrick Madigan and Madeleine Beaumont (Collegeville, Minnesota: The Liturgical Press, 1995).

In my own liturgical composition I have therefore sought to be deeply traditional in the sense that John Coltrane or James Joyce are traditional: I take melodies, tropes, stories and metaphors from the multiple religious traditions I have inherited and I remake them in a way that, I believe, will render their yearning toward the language of heaven real, concrete and reachable within the communicative community in which I am engaged. In most cases, this means that I render the ever-new surplus of communicative value inherent in the gospel event as a cultural stew or creole which resonates backwards and forwards at the same time. The prayers I compose are an improvisation on forms and themes familiar to any catholic Christian of the European kind. Yet much of the language is from a lower register and form of Australian English that is also sensitive to the landscape, seasons, and natural life of this continent in much the same way as the Psalmist or the author of the Song of Songs is sensitive to theirs.

Here is an example, a prayer of thanksgiving, lament and intercession penned for a recent conference of the Anglican diocese of Melbourne:

> In peace, let us pray to the Lord saying:
>
> Hear us, God of compassion,
> **and let our cry come unto thee.**
> We praise you for this ancient land, teaming with life:
> for Brolga, Emu and Turtle;
> for billabong, creek and waterways glistening;
> for desert and mountain and grassland through which your Spirit walks
> to make vitality explode into being;
> for ancestral spirits and people diverse and beautiful;
> for Christ your messenger, who tells the good news of your lovingkindness
> and casts it forth before you in his body broken and risen.
>
> God of the cross, many of us come before you with broken hearts this day,
> with hearts rent asunder by the breaking of ancient *makarrata*[7]
> written in country, kin and culture.

7. *Makarrata* is a word in the Yolngu language meaning a coming together after a struggle, facing the facts of wrongs and living again in peace according to a treaty or covenant.

We lament the wrecking of ancestral vocations, responsibilities,
stewardships.
We lament the stealing of land, of sea, of culture and kin.
We lament the violation of all that is sacred to those of us who have cared for this land
since time immemorial.

Hear us, God of compassion,
and let our cry come unto thee.

And so we pray for those kinspeople who are mourning today.
We remember the families of . . .
Comfort them all in their grief and, when the time is right,
raise up their faces and fill them with hopeful dreamings
full of lovingkindness and care.

Hear us, God of compassion,
and let our cry come unto thee.

We pray for our nation's leaders that, by treaty or covenant,
they may recognise the wise leadership of this country's most ancient peoples
for the good of everyone who now shares this commonwealth.
We pray for the leaders of our churches,
that we may embrace truth-telling and repentance concerning
our shared history
as the first steps toward the hope of a genuine reconciliation.

Hear us, God of compassion,
and let our cry come unto thee.

We pray for each other in all our diverse humanity,
that we may both delight and celebrate each other;
but also be prepared to care for each other,
to bear one another's burdens as Christ bears ours.
We lay before you our cares and pains for those whose lives have been crushed by poverty,
ill-health, or callous systems and workplaces.
In a moment of quiet prayer, we raise these dear ones in our hearts to you . . . .

Hear us, God of compassion,
and let our cry come unto thee.

Finally, God of love, we pray the prayer of the infant church:
veni sancte spiritus; Come, Holy Spirit!
Come, Holy Spirit, to heal our broken hearts.
Come, Holy Spirit, to heal our broken politics.
Come, Holy Spirit, to restore our broken relationships.
Come, Holy Spirit, to heal our broken churches and fill us with the dreamings of Jesus
for a world made new.
We long for the day when we shall sit at your banquet table
and share in your peace.

Hear us, God of compassion,
and let our cry come unto thee.

God of compassion, you have promised to hear our prayers.
And so we together offer the prayer that you taught your disciples:

Our Father in heaven . . .

This is a prayer that is deeply traditional in two directions: Europe and Gondwana. It reaches, at once, into the spiritual history of both Europe and Gondwana. It creates a dialogue between them through the use of analogy, symbol and metaphor. It does so in English, and yet the English has been 'queered' in a Gondwanan direction so that is no longer sounds exclusively colonial. The last section of this book offers a complete 'Eucharist for Gondwana' in the same spirit and using the same methodology.

Such queering is essential if we are to move beyond an unreconstructed colonial liturgy. Here we must think not only of written and spoken texts, but also of the liturgical environment: its sense of space and time. So, let's stop our exclusive use of white faces and white voices as we tell the story of faith on pewsheets and in storybooks and with projected images. Let's fill our churches with First People renderings of the biblical stories, in image, sculpture and soundscape. Let's write those stories as hybrid performances of *makarrata*, in altar frontals, in banners, in liturgical vestments. Let's stop arranging our churches like ancient Roman courthouses, the worshippers all facing the front where the 'holy things' and the 'holy people' are located. Let's place both the holy things and the holy elders in the midst of the holy assembly; let's face each other across a circle and bow towards the holy script of trinitarian life written upon our bodies and in our lives. Let's start using the incense, oils and aromas of the Australian bush in our rites of confession, lament, absolution and healing. Let's carry our baptismal water in vessels made from reed, rush and sea shell. Let's take our baptismal rites from the dark buildings of Europe, with their tiny fonts, and out to the more generous waters of river and sea. And let us compose new catechumenal rites that draw on the initiation rites of my people. If we do these things, we will render our liturgical performances more hospitable to the God who approaches and addresses us in the bodies and faces of First Peoples. And that can only be a good thing.

Chapter 3
The Unfinished Business of Reconciliation[1]

The word 'reconciliation' bears witness to a contested space within Indigenous Australia. For many, if not most, reconciliation is precisely what is needed in the face of the historic injustices visited upon Aboriginal peoples by the invading colonists who came to these lands from 1788 onward. Reconciliation describes a process by which colonists acknowledge, in detail, their wrongdoing and then seek forgiveness for these misdeeds from Australia's First Peoples. Importantly, for the proponents of reconciliation, absolution would not be automatic. It would be conditional upon Australia's colonising peoples making concrete and measurable efforts to undo previous evils or, in the many instances where such undoing is impossible, to offer a just and proportional compensation for wrongdoing in ways that meet the approval of First Peoples.

Is reconciliation a dirty word?

However, some Indigenous Australians are not at all happy with the language of reconciliation. They rightly point out that reconciliation is a Jewish and Christian idea, an idea that arrived with the colonists and cannot, therefore, be regarded as neutral or benign. For some Aboriginal commentators, the language of reconciliation is part of the colonising apparatus that keeps First Peoples 'down', and it does so by forcing Aboriginal and Torres Strait Islander people to think about their future within an alien framework that is not really their

1. An earlier version of this chapter was published as 'Reconciliation: personal reflections' in *Gesher: the official journal of The Council of Christians and Jews (Victoria) Inc.* 4/5 (2014): 16–19.

own, a framework that puts not their own, but colonists', interests at the centre. And what is the colonist's prevailing interest, according to this account? It is the need to find absolution, a salving of conscience, a healing of the gaping wound that has been rent in the colonial sense of self through its multitudinous breakings of the Jewish and Christian law: 'do not kill', 'do not steal', 'do not covet', 'do not bear false witness'. To this way of thinking, the colonial motivation for justice regarding First Peoples terminates not when Aborigines and Torres Strait Islanders are satisfied that justice has been done, but when the 'whitefella' sense of guilt is expiated. And that, quite simply, is not good enough.

In the brief paragraphs that follow, I should like to outline the way in which I, personally, have reconciled myself to the language of reconciliation. In doing so, I want my readers to know that that I was inducted by my parents and their community into the Baptist tradition of Christianity from a very young age. Since my childhood I have been keenly aware of a struggle, both within and without my person, between the British heritage of my Baptist beginnings and the trawloolway instinct for cultural survival against almost overwhelming odds. The nature of that struggle has often changed over the years. There have been times when I felt that my Christian heritage was indeed the enemy of all in me that is genuinely trawloolway, most often when the churchly institutions of Christianity steadfastly refused to recognise:

a) that I or my people are genuinely indigenous to this land: that we belong to this country, and the country belongs to us;
b) that I or my people are being, or have been, grievously mistreated or harmed through the ongoing violence of colonisation;
c) that churchly institutions participate, and have participated, in that mistreatment and harm;
d) that those same institutions therefore have a responsibility to make some kind of amends for the evils that have been visited upon my people.

In my view, churchly institutions have unfortunately made little progress on any of these fronts in my lifetime. Yes, fine words have been uttered in a very general way, especially by the Uniting Church to which I belonged for twenty-two years. But I still experience the church as fundamentally racist at the level of day-to-day, concrete relationships. It is in the wake of that experience of racism that I most often consider resigning both my membership and my holy orders in any form of historic Christian church.

At the same time, I have very often experienced the nascent Christianity into which I was inducted—represented, here, by its most fundamental language and imagination in Scripture and apostolic tradition—as the greatest ally I have in seeking to survive as a trawloolway man in colonial Australia. Consider, for example, the Pauline notion that God chooses the 'nothings' of this world—literally those who do not exist as far as the dominant powers are concerned—to be God's people and to 'shame' those who consider themselves wise and strong (1 Cor 1:26-31). As a person who has been repeatedly told throughout my life that I don't exist ('you are *not* Aboriginal, there *are* no Aboriginal Tasmanians left') or that I don't matter ('you *are* Aboriginal, but that means that you are a drunk, a welfare cheat, a waste of space and resources who has nothing meaningful to contribute') I find this notion deeply encouraging. Consider, also, Paul's revolutionary teaching about the identity of God. God, we are told in Scripture, was 'in Christ, reconciling the world to himself' (2 Cor 5:19). Yes, 'in Christ', a man despised, rejected, condemned to torture and crucifixion by the imperial powers of his world. In Christ, so the story goes, the creator of the universe exchanges his great power and position for that of a slave (Phil 2:6–7), that God might come close enough to offer help and salvation to all who are slaves, that God might lift them from their servitude to the colonising laws of sin and alienation and make them, instead, free children of God (Rom 8:15–17). Again, as one who has experienced the enslaving power of colonists, I am encouraged by this message about a God who is not identified with such power but comes, instead, *alongside* the colonised offering help, support and ultimately the gift of liberation. In my darkest moments, when I find myself agreeing with my oppressors that I am nothing, no one, of no value to anyone or anything, this message can be the only thing between me and oblivion. In this sense, the message of God's love that is at the heart of the Christian evangel is often the only thing that is able to rescue my trawloolway self from the overwhelmingly racist power of church and society alike.

Reconciliation as a language of truth with justice

So how have I reconciled myself to the language of reconciliation, a language that the colonists brought with them from over the seas? By, first, recognising that there can be no return to an existence or mode of Indigeneity that is somehow free of colonial influence, that dreams toward any such return are, ironically, generated by colonialism itself. And, then, by recognising the genuine power of the Christian gospel of reconciliation to make a positive difference to Indigenous people and not simply to our oppressors. And, finally, by recognising that the language of reconciliation in no way absolves colonists from shouldering the lion's share of responsibility when it comes to creating a just settlement for the First People's they have wronged. Indeed, as I will argue below, the language of reconciliation actually *creates* that responsibility. Allow me to expand on each of these claims in turn.

A few years ago I attended a conference on Wurundjeri country in Naarm/Melbourne that billed itself as a discussion of the notion of sovereignty from 'postcolonial' and 'theological' perspectives. The only Australian Indigenous speakers at the conference were a Warlpiri elder and his son, both of whom are also committed Baptists. Following their presentation, which drew liberally from the language of reconciliation, they were berated with questions about why, as Indigenous people, they felt the need to draw upon the 'language of the colonisers' at all. Did they not see that the language of reconciliation was little more than an opiate given to Aboriginal people by the missionaries as something of a consolation prize for the stealing of their lands and cultures? Why did they not draw, instead, on purely Indigenous stories and traditions in order to maintain their noble identities as Warlpiri people over and against the oppressive language of the coloniser? I found it extremely difficult to listen to these questions and take them seriously because, from my perspective, such questions serve only to inscribe the mentality and methods of colonialism all over again.

First, it is simply not possible to talk about a purely 'indigenous' language and tradition in contemporary Australia. The fact of contact between Indigenes and colonists over more than two hundred years has created new, more-or-less hybrid, narrative frameworks for the interpretation of Aboriginal and Torres Strait Islander traditions. That is what contact does: it creates new traditions out of older traditions. And the traditions live on precisely because they are living and adaptable; they are able to respond creatively to new data, new voices, new narratives and meaning structures. Every living First Nations culture in this country has adapted in this way. And every interpretation of older traditions—preserved, for example, in colonist's journals and academic papers—are themselves examples and performances of these hybrid narratives of contact between Indigenes and colonists. Any and all insistence about working from 'purely' Indigenous traditions—unpolluted by Western or Christian influences—is therefore not only naive but also deeply disrespectful of Indigenous people. It fails to recognise that it is precisely our ability to adapt and respond to colonial perspectives, to absorb them creatively into our own, that has made the difference between our surviving and not surviving.

Talk of cultural or racial 'purity' is also, rather nakedly in my view, a re-inscription of that 'noble savage'/Arcadian garden fantasy so beloved of Romantics and Nazis alike. The perseverance of the fantasy into 'postcolonial' (or, as I prefer, late-colonial) times demonstrates just how desperately the colonist needs to maintain the fiction that a 'pure' form of indigeneity is still possible. The fantasy has two basic functions. It first soothes colonial guilt by assuring the troubled conscience that the damage is not irreparable, the 'pure' has not, in fact, been irredeemably lost. At the same time, the fantasy also works to legitimate that familiar colonial strategy of dismissing or 'disappearing'—sometimes literally, sometimes figuratively (the effect is equally devastating in either case!)—all forms of the so-called 'half-caste' or 'half-breed'. Half-castes (so-called)—whether constructed in cultural or biological terms—are deeply threatening to colonists because they imply a 'muddying of the waters' regarding purist notions of identity, culture and vocation. Their presence, if acknowledged at all, signals the emergence of an alarming hybridity that deeply disturbs the 'us and them' dualism of the colonial psyche. It is a curious fact of colonial history around the world that colonists, usually from Europe, hate only one kind of people more than the 'blacks', and that is the 'coloureds'. It is my observation that settlers in Australia remain confused—routinely and predictably confused—by Indigenes like myself who do not fit their purist notions about what an Aboriginal person is. Settlers, whether their ancestry be European or Asian or something else, are routinely confronted and offended by the fact that the vast majority of Indigenous people in this country have fair skin and are clearly adept at living urban and suburban lives along with everyone else. In my personal experience, colonial masters are particularly offended by red-headed Aboriginal people who clearly know more about their traditions than they do themselves and are able to offer an alternative reading of the significance of those traditions from another place or viewpoint!

That brings me to my next point of reconciliation with the language of reconciliation: the genuine power of this narrative to make a positive difference, not only to oppressors, but also to Indigenous people. Against the critics of reconciliation who claim that the project is primarily about expiating 'white guilt' I want to say that reconciliation is actually about the truth, most of all—the telling of truth and the common ownership of that truth—by both First and settler peoples alike. The truth is this: that there can be no reconciliation, no coming together of First and settler peoples to build a more just future, without a common ownership of the undeniable truth of what has happened in this country.

For many years, from the 1820s right up until the 1990s, the public imagination of this country was dominated by a great silence about the stealing of Aboriginal lands and seas, the long war between invaders and native warriors, the systematic attempts to destroy whole cultures and nations, and the forced separation of Aboriginal and Torres Strait Islander children from their families. School children were taught that the land was largely 'empty' when white 'settlers' arrived and that the few natives who already lived here soon died out because of their stupidity and their failure to cultivate the land. Students were also taught that Australia was unique amongst European colonies because it had never known a war that was fought on its own soil.

These narratives were taught to Indigenes and colonists alike. But throughout this period First Peoples held on to our own histories, our own memories, our own versions of what had happened. Eventually our memories and tellings came to the attention of revisionist historians such as Manning Clarke, and later Lyndall Ryan, Bain Attwood and Henry Reynolds.[2] In their hands, the truth began to leach out into the public realm. It began to contest the false versions of history so

2. Manning Clarke, *History of Australia,* (Melbourne: Melbourne University Press, 1993); Lyndall Ryan, *The Aboriginal* Tasmanians, (Sydney: Allen and Unwin, 1996); Bain Attwood, *Possession: Batman's treaty and the matter of history,* (Melbourne: Melbourne University Press, 2009); Henry Reynolds, *The Other Side of the Frontier: Aboriginal resistance to the European invasion of Australia,* (Sydney: University of New South Wales Press, 1981).

beloved of those whose wealth and power had been founded on lies. As this truth is slowly owned by settlers, as the injustices visited upon Indigenous peoples and the fact of our survival slowly become part of a common national narrative, a more genuine launching-place for a reconciled future comes into focus. For reconciliation begins, as the Johannine tradition says, with a confession of the truth (1 John 1:8). Without the recognition of that truth, there can be no freedom (John 8:32). For freedom, in this understanding, is ultimately about liberation from falsehood and lies; lies about oneself, about others, and about the identity of the divine. Whoever lives in falsehood is a slave to falsehood. But whoever is set free from falsehood by the arrival of the truth will be free to choose a new destiny (Jn 8:34–38).

Perhaps it is now clear why I feel compelled to argue that the language of reconciliation *in no way* absolves colonists from shouldering the lion's share of responsibility when it comes to creating a just settlement for the First Peoples they have wronged. Indeed, as I have already intimated, the language of reconciliation actually *creates* that responsibility. For wrongdoing, in the language of reconciliation, creates a responsibility in the guilty party to provide satisfaction or recompense to the party that has been wronged.

How did Jacob reconcile himself to Esau, the brother whom he had wronged by swindling him out of his inheritance? First he confessed to God that he was, in truth, unworthy of the good fortune that had come his way (Gen 32:10). Then he sent a very valuable 'gift' on ahead of him—a great flock of goats, sheep, camels, cattle and donkeys—along with a message that these were for Esau (Gen 32:13-21). When the two brothers finally meet, Esau greets Jacob with words of forgiveness and grace, to be sure, but the story is structured in such a way as to highlight Jacob's responsibility to offer—at least to offer!—some kind of compensation for what had clearly been stolen. A saying of Jesus in St Matthew's version of the Sermon on the Mount reinforces the point. If one attends the temple to be reconciled to God, one should not pretend that such reconciliation is going to be in any way real or effective if there is a matter outstanding between oneself and another. If you have wronged someone, Jesus counsels, you must first do whatever it takes to be reconciled with that person before you can pretend to seek the forgiveness of God (Matt 5:23–24).

So, while the language of reconciliation clearly invokes the possibility of forgiveness as a way through to a lasting peace, the granting of forgiveness is very often conditional: conditional upon a recognition in the guilty parties that they have indeed done wrong, and that those parties therefore have a responsibility to make recompense for what has been stolen or destroyed.[3]

A call to Church leaders

Let me conclude with a challenge for the Christian leaders who will read this chapter. Can any of you say, out of the truth that whispers deep in your hearts,[4] that you have truly taken responsibility for the wrongs your churches and congregations have visited upon the First Peoples of this land? Have you acknowledged your part in stealing land, removing children, and destroying culture? Have you acknowledged, and do you take responsibility for, the ongoing effects of these injustices in the form of disproportionately high levels of Indigenous poverty, incarceration, physical and mental illness? Furthermore, have you made an apology to the people so affected—not in that general rhetorical way so beloved of politicians and CEOs—but face-to-face, neighbour-to-neighbour? Have you demonstrated to the people you have wronged that you are serious about seeking recompense and justice for them, so that they may have a chance to create a better future? Have you asked them what form that recompense should take, genuinely asked them? Have they been given a seat at the table in terms of leadership and the setting of denominational policy? Have you begun to renew or replace your unjust institutions in the light of what you are learning?[5] For the

3. Elsewhere I have explored in detail the relationship between what has been called the 'conditional' and 'unconditional' dimensions of covenant-making in the Jewish and Christian traditions. I am aware that unconditional forgiveness very often creates the possibility for a just response in the wrongdoer. My intent in this essay is not to exclude that possibility outright, but simply to argue that whatever the motivation toward just compensation, recompense is always part of the settlement phenomenologically. See Garry J. Deverell, *The Bonds of Freedom: Vows, Sacraments and the Formation of the Christian Self* (Milton Keynes, UK: Paternoster Press, 2008) pp. 124–127.
4. For a sustained exegesis of this phrase from Richard Windeyer, see Henry Reynolds, *This Whispering in our Hearts* (St Leonards, NSW: Allen & Unwin, 1998).
5. Daniel Philpott proposes that any form of genuine reconciliation must include the establishment of more just institutions, for institutions are the primary way in which practices are stabilised in law and civil society. See *Just and Unjust Peace: An Ethic of Political Reconciliation* (New York: Oxford University Press, 2012).

history of do-gooders in this country unfortunately suggests that such asking, and the careful listening for a guiding response that is part of any genuine partnership, rarely happens on the ground. Instead, it is the colonists who decide what form the compensation should take, and when, and how. Your response to these questions will make all the difference to whether reconciliation really has a chance in Australia, or whether it does not. My prayer, as always, is that the veil of ignorance might be torn from all our eyes (2 Cor 4:4). Only then will reconciliation have a chance.

In the Church, as in the whole of society, it is especially important that Indigenous Christians are permitted to order our own affairs. I have argued already, in these brief chapters, for the recognition of First Nations ways of being Christian, of worshipping God, of being church. Our ways are not necessarily for everyone, but they are our ways nevertheless. If the colonial church could get to a point of understanding and accepting this situation, we would be very happy indeed. As it is, colonial churches appear to persist in the view that they know what is best for us, and that 'best' turns out to be—surprise, surprise!—the 'best' that pertains to the dominant imagination and culture, derived largely from Europe. Recompense for the church in Australia will certainly involve allowing its First Peoples to 'do' Christianity in our own way: to set up our own self-governing presbyteries, dioceses and synods; to worship and theologise in ways that honour our dreaming alongside the inherited traditions of Europe; to evangelise our people, as well as the wider community, according to the accent in which *we* hear the call of the Spirit. That is what we have been trying to do for 200 years and more, usually in the face of stiff and often violent resistance from the colonial powers who run the churches. Whether those churches will repent and become part of a new future for us all—a future in which Indigenous Christians are no longer invisible and silent but welcomed as creative contributors to a renewal of the whole church out of the lessons of our own history and experience with God—remains an open question.

Chapter 4
On Racism and the Trinity[1]

For a number of years now, an increasing number of Australians have been observing the week of May 27 to June 3 as 'Reconciliation Week'. Bookended by the annual commemorations of the 1967 referendum and the Mabo decision in the High Court, the week is used, in various ways and by various groups, to promote reconciliation and peace between First Peoples and those who came here more latterly from across the sea. In 2013 there was a focus on the continuing scourge of racism. For who can doubt that racism is still very much amongst us? The exchange between a football fan and dual Brownlow medallist Adam Goodes at the Sydney/Collingwood game on May 24 of that year—when Mr Goodes was branded an 'Ape'—is a powerful reminder of that fact. It is also a fact that our national constitution still pretends that Aboriginal people have no power in our own land. It is a thoroughly racist document in that it fails to recognise that Australia was not an 'empty land' when the Europeans came; that it had been inhabited and cultivated by another people for at least 60 thousand years, that it was taken from that people by force, and without lawfully recognised treaty, and that the effects of this taking are still amongst us in the form of disturbing levels of social, psychological and spiritual trauma amongst Indigenous people. As a trawloolway man, I know about the effects of colonisation 'up close and personal', as they say. The way I look at everything—the landscape, society, the church, political and theological ideas—is profoundly influenced by that inter-generational experience of trauma, loss and survival.

1. This chapter began life as three reflections posted on my blog at uncommonprayers.blogspot.com, namely 'Fellow Heirs Through the Gospel', 'On Aboriginality' and 'Your Pain Will Turn to Joy'.

Racism is not just an academic category for me. It is something I encounter in conversation and relationship. I will share just two stories. At lunch a few years ago with a group of intelligent, sophisticated, ordained presbyters, the talk turned towards the role of Aboriginal and Torres Strait Islander people in our church. Suddenly the talk became less intelligent and less sophisticated. These people, whom I knew and respected, suddenly started to caricature, stereotype, and make fun of Aboriginal people in a way that seemed to contradict everything else they believed in. The apparent fun of this turn in the conversation was far from fun for me. Indeed, I felt deeply wounded by what was said, so wounded that I was stunned into a tumultuous silence so confusing that I found myself unable to say anything to them about either how I was feeling or about the substance of what they were doing. Now, those who know me well will tell you that I am rarely short of things to say, especially if I catch a whiff of injustice somewhere. So, this was a really strange and bewildering experience for me. It had been a very long time since I had felt that fearful, that powerless, and that small. But that is what racist taunts do to a person. They make you feel as though you are not a human being. They bring home to you the tragic fact that there are people in the world who believe that you are unworthy of the respect they would normally extend to other human beings, simply because you belong, in some way, to a category of existence that is other than their own.

And another story. On April 3 2013, I went for a drive with my wife's extended family in northeast Tasmania along the coast road between leenerrerterer country (Bridport) and tebrikunna (Musselroe Bay), where we were able to clearly see the islands of the Furneaux group to the immediate north. This is a part of the state that I love very much, not least because it is my ancestral home. I am a direct descendent of the clans who lived their lives along this coastline for more than 35 thousand years prior to European occupation.

As we sped past the sacred mountain, poonerluttener (Mt Cameron), where the clans traditionally gathered for trade, council and sacred ceremony, one member of the family initiated a conversation about a live dispute between his local church and the neighbouring Aboriginal Centre about the placement of a fence. He observed that the Aboriginal community in question was probably made up of people who had come from other parts of the state, because 'there were no Aborigines in our town when the settlers arrived'. I informed him that there were a number of Deverells involved in the palawa community in his town, to which he responded (and I quote), 'Oh, the Deverells are as Aboriginal as I am'. Since this family member's ancestry is strictly European, I assume that what he meant by this is that the Deverells, myself included, are not really Indigenes of Tasmania at all and that our claims to the contrary are therefore spurious at best. I confess that I was rendered quite speechless. Which, as I have already written, is not a condition I am used to. Not at all.

This incident raised, yet again, a question I have been dealing with my whole life. In what sense can a white-skinned and red-headed lad from Sheffield, Tasmania—who, incidentally, happens to have an Irish-Norman family name—claim to be Aboriginal? If Aboriginality is not primarily about the colour of one's skin and the keeping-intact of traditional notions of blood, culture and habitation, then what could possibly remain? I will not rehearse here the history of colonialism in Tasmania. Others have done that very well, Lyndall Ryan, Ian McFarlane and James Boyce amongst them. I simply want to repeat that contemporary Aboriginal identity is not primarily about the dominance of a particular biological inheritance over and against others. Nor is it about the preservation of a pre-colonial, 'tribal', way of life. Aboriginal identity is about the perseverance of a sense of Indigenous being—embedded in a deeply ontological sense of belonging to kin and country—over and against the will of a dominant culture and society that has systematically sought to erase these things. Given the devastating success of the colonising will, especially in places like Tasmania and Victoria, this means that Aboriginality is most often preserved in the form of a memory and a deep-down sorrow pertaining to what has been broken or stolen—land, kin, dreaming—a sorrow that is manifested in various forms of grief and mourning, but also in the search for a justice in which these things might be returned or, at least, partially recovered.

My own Aboriginal identity is manifested, I believe, in the way I look at the Tasmanian landscape. What I see and the way I see it is very, very different to the way in which my in-laws see it. As we drove along the coast road that day, that member of my wife's family very often spoke of the productivity of the farmland, the breed of the dairy-herds, the people he knew who were, or had been, engaged in the mining and farming of the land. He spoke with the pride of a family that had come from the other side of the world and made itself prosperous by the sweat of its collective brow. It was a discourse of celebration and pride that was quite blind to the history and experience of my own people who lost that same land at the point of a gun. Some have called it 'white-blindness', a learned incapacity to see and feel what is clearly there to be seen and felt because of an ethnic filter that is constantly, albeit unconsciously, employed to reduce the complexity of any given interaction.[2]

What I saw and felt on that afternoon drive could not be more different. I saw a land that was filled with older memories. At each creek I imagined a small group of women searching for swan's eggs, woven baskets around their shoulders. At each open plain I saw men chasing kangaroos and wallabies with spears, waddys and firesticks. As we passed poonerluttener I imagined the ecstasy of dancing, the shrewdness of trade, the skill of legal and theological storytelling and dispute. When we stopped by the bay, I saw women diving for shellfish, and fires on the beach around which families gathered to consume stories and news along with their food. I also felt the loss of these things: the drying-up of food stocks as invaders pushed up the rivers; the hunting and stealing of people and of land; the agonizing deaths wrought by new diseases. I looked across the straits at the Islands and saw the devastation on my ancestor Mannarlagenna's face as he realised he was being consigned, along with the peers he had sought to rescue from the white scourge, to the world of the dead.

This is a sensibility that I wish I could successfully share with my in-laws and the wider community. I have tried to do so in various ways across a number of years. But I fear I have failed, for the look of incomprehension so often remains, even after telling my stories many times over. White-blindness, it seems, is all-pervasive. As such, it remains the deepest and most intractable form of racism. And for those of us who encounter is regularly, it is simply exhausting. Having to explain your very existence over and over again depletes the soul.

---

2. For more on 'whiteness' theory see Cheryl I. Harris, 'Critical Characteristics of Whiteness as Property' in *Harvard Law Review* 109:1709-1721 (1993); Ruth Frankenberg, *White Women, Race Matters: The Social Construction of whiteness*, 5th edition (Minneapolis: University of Minnesota Press, 1993); Radhika Mohanram, *Imperial White: Race, Diaspora, and the British Empire* (Minneapolis: University of Minnesota Press, 2007); Theodore W Allen, *The Invention of the White Race*, volumes 1 & 2 (London: Verso, 2012).

It is deeply interesting to me that the Christian Feast of the Holy Trinity often occurs within Reconciliation Week. This is a day when Christians reflect explicitly on themes that are regrettably much more implicit during the rest of the year: namely the nature and mission of God as a trinitarian communion of three *persona*, the 'Father', the 'Son' and the 'Holy Spirit'. The lections set down for Trinity Sunday seek to encourage such reflection. A reading from Proverbs (8:1–4, 22–31) speaks of 'Wisdom' as if she were a person, a person who cannot be simply separated from God as yet another of God's myriad creations. Wisdom is here spoken of as the very 'first' of God's possessions, appointed 'from eternity', begotten of God rather than created out of nothing. Furthermore, Wisdom is both a witness and co-worker with God in the act of creating the universe, a master craftswoman at Yahweh's side. It is clear that many early Christian theologians understood this passage, and its sister passages in the apocryphal *Book of Wisdom*, as Jewish presentiments concerning Jesus Christ. We are all familiar with the opening poem at the beginning of John's gospel:

> In the beginning was the Word, and the Word was with God, and the Word was the same as God. He was in the beginning with God. All things came into being through him, and without him not one thing came into being. What has come into being in him was life, and that life was the light of all people . . . The true light, which enlightens everything, was coming into the world (Jn 1:1–9).

Like Wisdom, the Word exists in the beginning with God and shares in the divine action of creating. The Word, like Wisdom, may be understood as some kind of emanation from God. The Word, in other words, is born of God, not made by God out of non-divine material. And finally, like Wisdom, the Word is imagined as a divine light which enlightens the world. Much recent scholarship concludes that Lady Wisdom is the model out of which John created the divine *logos* which became, in short order, the second person of the Trinity, the divine Son. The Son shares in the deity of the Father, but cannot be absolutely identified with the Father, certainly not without remainder.

Look at John's careful treatment of the relationship between the Father and the Son in another of the lections for Trinity Sunday (Jn 16:12–23). 'All that belongs to the Father is mine', says Jesus. He also says, 'My Father will give you anything you ask for in my name'. Names are important in the New Testament imagination. Names represent a person who is not present. They are the same as the person themselves, yet they are different from that person also, because they can stand for, or represent, that person in their absence. So, when Jesus says 'The Father will give you anything you ask for in my name', what he is really saying is this: 'I am the exact representation and presence of my Father. If you cannot see the Father physically, yet, in looking upon me and listening to my voice you can see and hear the Father, for everything I am, I received from my Father, and everything the Father is has been given to me. So, ask in my name. To do so is ask of my Father what I have already been given you in me'. According to John, Jesus of Nazareth is the same as the pre-existent Word of God who was begotten of God the Father before the creation of the world and shares in his Father's deity and power; in Jesus we therefore see and hear all that we can, as human beings, see and hear of God. Jesus is the paradigm occurrence of Father's face and arms and voice for the material world of flesh and blood in which we live and move and have our human being.

What of the Holy Spirit, then? Well, according to John once more, the Spirit clearly shares in the divine being of the Father and the Son. Jesus says that the Spirit will come once he, the flesh-and-blood Christ, has passed from this world. The Spirit will guide the disciples into the truth of God, a truth the Spirit will repeat and echo into our human hearts exactly as it is spoken in the life of God, in the divine conversation between the Father and the Son. The Spirit possesses everything that the Father and the Son possess. The Spirit shares in the divine being of the Father and the Son, but also in the relationship of non-identity they share with each other. Some theologians have speculated that the Spirit *is* the relationship between the Father and the Son, the very intangibility of their love and regard for each other, the substance of their conversation and their care. That may well be true, for the Spirit is indeed less 'solid' than the Father and the Son in terms of character and identity. The Spirit is a tad more wild and mysterious in her workings, like a wind that comes from nowhere and goes to nowhere. And yet, what she brings us from her divine companions is something very valuable indeed: truth, hope and joy. She is the midwife of these things, John tells us, the one who assures us that they are real and that they will one day belong to us, even as we weep and grieve and labour in this valley of tears we call the world.

A Trinity lection from St Paul in Romans makes a similar point (5:1–5). It makes the claim that all who believe in Jesus Christ and have received the justification that comes from him as a free gift of grace, have also received the gift of the Holy Spirit, who is nothing other than the vessel in which the love and mercy of God arrive. This gift, says the Apostle, gives us hope when life is difficult. She helps us to rejoice when there is little to rejoice about. She helps us to persevere and to be disciplined in the face of difficult circumstances. For the promise is there for all who believe, that our pain will turn to joy and that our weeping will one day turn into laughter.

Now, it is unfortunately true that around our churches today there will be a great many sermons that skip over the feast of the Trinity and over trinitarian theology in general, because so many of our preachers simply do not have the wisdom or the wit to know what to do with it. Many, unfortunately, see the doctrine of the Trinity as something of an irrelevance, an ancient curiosity that really has nothing to say to our contemporary world or faith. Nothing, of course, is further from the truth. What such preachers fail to appreciate it that the doctrine of the Trinity, like all doctrine, is a story. A story of God, and God's dealings with the world of human beings that unleashes the power to transform our despair into joy, our hearts of stone into hearts of flesh and feeling. The doctrine of the Trinity is shorthand, in other words, for everything the Christian faith has to offer by way of truth, justice, faith and hope. It is the grammar out of which we may start to comprehend our world, our society and our church as the arena of God's action for forgiveness, justice and peace. It is the divine *mythos* through which we might answer even the most puzzling of our human questions.

'Why is racism evil?' for example. Have you ever even asked yourself that question? What story, what grammar, do we depend upon to render the denigration of another person (on the basis of nothing more than their skin colour or ethnic profile) as fundamentally wrong, false, evil, immoral? The usual way of answering the question, in contemporary Australia, is that racism is evil because human beings are equally deserving of respect and care, whatever their ethnicity: which I agree with. But what if one were to then ask, 'but why are human beings equally deserving of respect and care'? That is a question that many Australians find much more difficult to answer, I suspect (not that we ask ourselves the question very much at all).

I know this because Australians of the most dominant, Northern European, sort seem to put their prohibitions concerning racism aside when it suits them, which says to me that deep down many of them don't really know why racism is so very wrong. Why did the Cronulla rioters of December 2005 chant racist slogans and beat each other up? Why did the Aussie cricket fans at the Melbourne and Sydney tests of that same year make racist remarks towards the South African bowler Makhaya Ntini? Why does our government continue to lock up asylum seekers in concentration camps on Manus and Nauru, when there is no evidence of their having committed any crime against this state? Because, deep down, many Australians do not believe that the ethical injunction against racism is absolute. They believe, rather, that the prohibition can be put aside when it suits them, when something more important comes along, like wanting to defeat or belittle a person or a group or a team that are perceived, for one reason or another, to be a threat.

So much for the secular imagination. For Christians, however, the answer to the question 'why is racism evil?' is the doctrine of the Trinity. The Father sends the Son into the world of flesh and blood in order to show us how to live justly, to reveal to us what is right and what is wrong, what makes for life and what makes for death. In the face of the Son we learn that God does this out of an infinite love for 'the world', for us all (cf. John 3:16). God longs for our life, not our death, for our flourishing, not our diminishing. In the face of Christ, we learn that God is no bully, but is prepared to come amongst us in the vulnerable form of the Son, to remonstrate and plead with us, that we might choose the way to life. God does this even to the point of being misunderstood or, conversely, understood very well, but ultimately rejected. Even to the point of death, death on a cross. Not that death can kill God's love, for in the power of the Spirit the Son is raised to life as a sign of hope that all who follow in Christ's way will themselves be raised, will themselves transcend death's dominion when the racists and the death-squads come to exact their terrible revenge.

So, racism is evil because God the creator is a communion of love since all eternity, and wants to include everyone, without remainder—whatever their skin colour or ethnic origin—at the table of mercy and hospitality shared forever by the Father, the Son and the Holy Spirit. Racism is evil because God is willing to put everything on the line in Jesus Christ—and, through the Spirit, also within the very human and therefore fragile history of the church—in order to make that message resonate loud and clear within the arena of our inhumanity toward one another. Racism is evil, finally, because it will not have the last word. The last word is love, the love shared between the Father and the Son in the power of the Holy Spirit, a love that is always going out of itself in creative and hospitable action. In the gift of Christ, we who believe are empowered to rejoice in the final victory of that love even as the evil of racism continues to permeate our world. For the Spirit is a deposit, a guarantee of that which is to come: a sign in our midst of that final peace-making, the *shalom* of God, when all who are reconciled to God are also reconciled to one another. In the work of Christ and the giving of his Spirit, every sin is both forgiven and forgotten and the idea that someone might be used and abused because of their ethnicity has become absolutely laughable. Racism is evil, in summary, because God is a trinity, a threefold relation of divine equals who go out toward one another and toward the cosmos in love and mercy. In this story and this grammar is the indispensable plumbline of care and regard and justice . . . for the church, for human society, and for the whole of creation.[3]

3. I acknowledge a profound debt, in this chapter, to the thinking of Brazilian theologian Leonardo Boff, especially his *Trinity and Society* (Tunbridge Wells: Burns and Oats, 1988).

Chapter 5
A Letter to my First Nations Kin Concerning the Church

The implied audience of this book so far has been broad, addressing both First Peoples and settlers. Now I want to specifically address my Aboriginal and Torres Strait Islander kin. First, I want to offer some sobering observations from my own experience about the capacity of the church to engage in a genuine process of reconciliation with us. I'd like to explore *why it is* that the Australian churches, despite their many grand statements to the contrary, seem so incapable of keeping their hearts and their budgets focussed on the goals of justice and right relationship with our people. After that, I'd like to shift the focus onto our own communities for a moment and ask if there is anything lurking in our *own hearts and minds* that might be undermining our aspirations for a more just peace with the church. To what extent, I shall ask, have we so internalised the racism of our society that we no longer believe that we deserve a better deal, a better settlement, a treaty that recognises our preeminent sovereignty in this country and its seas and its churches? Finally, I'd like to make some modest suggestions about the way in which we might seek to *reset the relationship* with our churches in such a way that the urgency of reconciliation can no longer be ignored.

My story with the church

My pilgrimage with the churches and reconciliation began when I was a naïve, and highly idealistic, young candidate for ministry with the Baptist Union of Tasmania. It was 1993 and the Tasmanian government had just proposed its Aboriginal Lands Act, in which a few parcels of land—mostly of symbolic rather than practical value—would be returned to the palawa community. This move was unprecedented in the Tasmanian community, representing something of a revolution in the wake of 190 years of consistently genocidal policy settings. The churches, especially the 'free' churches, responded with a resounding silence. So, I wrote a piece for the local Baptist press in which I suggested that Christians of every stripe, being followers of the Jesus who represented God's radical love for the most poor and marginalised, ought to be vocal supporters of the government's proposals. The most immediate effect of my intervention was a barrage of letters, addressed both to me and to senior Baptist leaders, criticising the article for its both its unsound representation of the ministry of Jesus and its 'black armband' rendering of history. The volume of the letters received was enough to convince the denominational leaders that my suitability for ordination in Tasmania should be called into question. Within a year, by mutual agreement, I had resigned my candidacy. My relationship with the church was officially at an all-time low.

Since that time, I have sought to engage with two more national churches about the need for a more just settlement for my people. In 1997, as a newly-ordained presbyter of the Uniting Church, I was sent from Melbourne back to Tasmania, to a provincial city only half an hour's drive from my home town. The local Aboriginal people there were my own mob—almost all them descendants, like me, of Dolly Dalrymple—and I quickly sought to broker a process by which the local churches in Devonport might offer an apology for past practices and commit themselves to an ongoing relationship with my mob, which sought after a greater justice, a more adequate recompense, a deeper healing for all my people. Things began well. We found a form of words that was acceptable to our elders as well as to the local church leaders. We gathered at the meeting place of the Mersey-Leven Aboriginal Corporation (as it was then called). The words were said. There was a gracious response. The local newspaper ran a story. But then the whole thing petered out. Indeed, when I sought to revisit the apology on Sorry Day in the following year by inviting church leaders to examine what they were doing *right now* to give body and substance to their apology, most simply ignored the call but some came back at me with considerable hostility. I remember the local Assembly of God pastor coming to my house to say, and I summarise, 'We've said sorry, so there is nothing else to do; our relationship with

God has been restored'. As if being right with God could *ever* bypass the relationship with one's neighbour! At the Sorry Day worship service I sought to organise for churches along the north-west coast, with the aid of an interview on ABC radio and newly-arrived communication technologies like email, only a few faithful souls felt the need to gather. If memory serves well, out of all the churches of north-west Tasmania, half of them from my own congregation.

Around the same time, the Tasmanian Synod of the Uniting Church had a debate about whether the national Church should issue an apology concerning the involvement of its predecessor denominations in the systematic removal of First Nations children from their families as agents of multiple Australian governments over 150 years. I remember being at that meeting and listening to multiple speakers stand to either defend the practice outright or minimise the church's culpability on the grounds of a naïve innocence about what was 'really going on'. Honestly, the whole debate resonated with the trials at Nuremburg following the second world war. Those of us who represented the Uniting Aboriginal and Islander Christian Congress kept our eyes lowered. We wept. We struggled for composure. All of us, all of our families, had been traumatised by the removals in ways that continued to impact our health and well-being across multiple generations. When we were asked to speak, it was difficult to do so coherently. The speeches we had already heard brought home to us just how far the church had to go in coming to terms with its complicity in the genocide of our people. I am referring, of course, to the real church: the church on the ground in congregations rather than the one that crafts fine words in the corporate offices of Sydney or Melbourne. We felt our personal integrity was being violated all over again. And the power of speech—at least that mode of speech acceptable within the value-system of the audience we had to address—simply deserted us.

There were many other blows to my idealism over the years that followed, blows that will be familiar to you, my First Nations kin. On multiple occasions the church—Anglican, Catholic, Uniting—organised forums or committees on justice and reconciliation for First Nations people to which only the most easily 'managed' First Nations people were invited. You know, the ones who will not rock the boat. The ones with the blackest skin and the least education in Western ways. The 'mission' people. The ones whose analyses of the *ongoing* racism of the church are least likely to be heard and taken seriously. Please understand what I am saying here. I don't *blame* mission people for accepting such invitations. I don't blame them for *being* mission people. Who they are, and how they think, is as much a product of colonisation as my own pink skin and revolutionary tendencies. But the church is very clever in the ways it includes and excludes, in the ways it plays us off against each other, in the ways it shames us for speaking our truth when the mode of that speech does not conform to nice, white and middle-class, modes of address. The church remains a very clever mission-manager, even though most of the missions are no more.

For all their fine words of the past twenty years or so, for all their apologies and grand statements about being 'committed' to justice and to reconciliation with the First Peoples of Australia, the churches remain largely inactive when it comes to doing anything practical about the big-ticket items on our First Nations agenda. We remain largely unrepresented in the most senior leadership forums of the church, at both national and provincial levels. Without the opportunity to offer a clear and consistent First Nations voice within the most important policy-making bodies of our churches, our aspirations for recompense and a more just settlement will, quite simply, remain at the very bottom of the agenda (if they get on the agenda at all). Not surprisingly, then, the forms of 'reconciliation' the church will come at are the *least costly* ones: conferences, forums, special liturgical events, talk-fests. The *more costly* gestures—in both a moral and economic sense—remain seriously under-done: positive employment targets, accompanied by a substantial investment in First Nations staff and students within our training institutions; a commitment to funding First Nations theologians and theological reflection as a matter of first priority for the Australian churches; the activation of real targets for the return of stolen property to First Nations control in order to provide an economic base for ministry with, by, and for First Nations people; the reorientation of diocesan or synodical budgets towards an ongoing work of restitution and recompense towards First Nations people (in a way that is perhaps analogous to the way in which the church is finally compensating its many thousands of sexual abuse victims); the creation of new, more just, institutions. Until the churches engage in these costlier forms of reconciliation, their words will remain hollow.

It is sobering to note that, in twenty-five years of public ministry as a First Nations pastor, I have publicly shared something of the story of my people only nine times with a gathered group of non-Indigenous Christians. The earliest invitations came from the wonderful Sisters of St Joseph in Tasmania. They first asked me to tell my story at their annual convocation in 1998. A year later one of their number organised a series of ecumenical gatherings on King Island at which I was able to preach in church but also share a little of the story of the Stolen Generations at the local school. The next occasion came soon after we moved back to Wurundjeri country in Victoria, in around 2002. The leaders of our own local UCA church in Clayton asked me to share something of what I knew about the Aboriginal history of Melbourne as they sought to prepare a plaque acknowledging the traditional custodians. Eight years after that, as part of a day spent at Narana (the UAICC facility on Wathaurong country in Geelong) I was asked to share some of my nativist theological musings with a group of ministry students who, incidentally, responded with great interest. The final five opportunities to share my story have all happened in the last year! Twice my own Anglican parish in Mt Waverley asked me to speak, along with the Anglican parishes of St Michael's, North Carlton, and St Oswald's, Glen Iris. And the Australian Network of Spiritual Directors asked me to share some reflections on 2017's 'Statement from the Heart' at a professional development day in Malvern.

The 'why?' question: why has reconciliation with the churches barely taken flight?

My pilgrimage with the churches has often caused me to ask the 'why' question: Why, after all the historians have now taught us about dispossession and the frontier wars; after all the national enquiries into phenomena such as the stolen generations and Aboriginal deaths in custody; after all the research demonstrating that First Nations people continue to bear the scars of colonisation as much today as ever; why does the yawning abyss between the rhetoric of reconciliation in the churches and its concrete practice on the ground still remain? That question becomes even more puzzling when one remembers that the very *raison d'être* of the churches is to be communities of reconciliation that continually proclaim, in word and deed, the good news of God's transforming mercy and forgiveness in Christ to the whole creation. If any community should be leading the way through a process of truth and justice to reconciliation with First Peoples, if any community should be lighting the path for the rest of the nation, it is the churches. Yet, in Australia, the churches do not *lead* society to salvation, they *follow* it . . . very often, at a distance of decades! So why? Why are the churches so backward in coming forward, on this issue especially?

The answer lies, I think, in the close collaboration between church and state in the prosecution of this nation's most original sin: the dispossession of its First Peoples and the genocidal policies that remained in place for close to 150 years thereafter. From the beginning, the churches were willing instruments of the state in removing us from our land; in promoting the damaging ideology of the Arcadian savage which ended up dividing us from one another according to the proto-Nazi notion of caste (or degrees of whiteness), and in the wholesale destruction of our languages and our cultures. There were, and are, exceptions of course. But the people who worked to preserve our ways did so within a machinery and an ideology intent on genocide. So their high-minded efforts for good often turned out, tragically, to serve evil instead. There is an echo, here, of St Paul's account of the struggle between 'flesh' and 'Spirit':

> For we know that the law is spiritual; but I am of the flesh, sold into slavery under sin. I do not understand my own actions. For I do not do what I want, but I do the very thing I hate. Now if I do what I do not want, I agree that the law is good. But in fact it is no longer I that do it, but sin that dwells within me. For I know that nothing good dwells within me, that is, in my flesh. I can will what is right, but I cannot do it. For I do not do the good I want, but the evil I do not want is what I do. Now if I do what I do not want, it is no longer I that do it, but sin that dwells within me. So I find it to be a law that when I want to do what is good, evil lies close at hand (Rom 7:14–21).

The churches are unable to 'do the right thing' regarding our people, in my view, because the original sin in which they were willingly enrolled upon coming to this country continues to structure their thoughts and actions at a deeply unconscious level. Even though the churches know very well what they ought to do, they do not do it because it would cost them too much: it would cost them their most precious fantasy about being 'good' people, 'ethical' people, people who can be relied on to love as Jesus loved. Doing the right thing would require the churches to confess that their place and privilege in this country was stolen, taken by illegitimate means on the basis of a fiction, the fiction of *terra nullius*. Doing the right thing would require the churches to admit that they have been the direct beneficiaries of dispossession and, further, that what has been stolen really ought, according to the law of both Moses and Jesus, be given back. Doing the right thing would also mean altering the power-structures of the church in a root-and-branch manner, so that First Peoples can take our legitimate place at the table. Given the choice between, on the one hand, telling the truth about what has happened and doing as the law of Christ requires and, on the other, continuing to live within a complex and nuanced fantasy concerning their own righteousness, the churches choose the latter. And they do so repeatedly.

The third possible option intimated by the Apostle remains, in all but the most exceptional instances, the way not taken:

> Wretched man that I am! Who will rescue me from this body of death? Thanks be to God through Jesus Christ our Lord! (Rom 7:24–25).

The third way is the way of self-emptying love. It is the way of Jesus Christ, who, though he had a share in divinity itself, emptied himself and became a slave who died the most ignoble of deaths, death on a cross. All 'for us, and for our salvation' as the ecumenical creed says. There is nothing magic in the Christian doctrine of atonement. It is not, in the end, about an economic transaction in the heavens by which our debt of sin is bought by a third party, a kinsman-redeemer named Jesus. It is about the extraordinary love of the kinsman-redeemer for his wretched family. It is about the way in which he is willing to shoulder the burden of our wretchedness for as long as it takes for us to crawl out from underneath the folly of our self-destruction. In love, there is no room for either self-justification or self-righteousness. In Christ, we encounter not a judgy God who stands above us in irreproachable purity and calls us to get our act together but, rather, a companion God who leaves all such security behind in order to get beside and even underneath us, forever encouraging and empowering us to take just the next step toward the distant light.

The point I am making with regard to the churches is this: 'freely you have received, freely give' (Matt 10:8). As Christ has given himself freely for our salvation—counting neither the cost, nor our sins against us—so the churches are called to give themselves freely for the salvation of those against whom they have sinned most grievously, namely ourselves, the First Peoples. A church that did this would care not a fig how much it cost. It would not be concerned about the 'damage' to its reputation or its future viability as an economic or social entity. It would simply pour itself out to help and heal its victims. And by losing itself so—such is the mystery at the heart of the gospel—it would actually recover itself anew as the church, the body of Christ, given for the life of the world. I continue to have faith that such a church might arise from the ashes of Australian colonialism. But, faith being 'the assurance of things hoped for, the conviction of things not seen' (Heb11:1), I live, for the foreseeable future, with the reality of a church that is not yet ready to follow the way of Jesus.

How ought we engage with such a church?

This begs the question: How ought we, as First Peoples who happen to be Christians, engage with a such a church? How are we to go on being part of the church, when the church seems so incapable of recognising and accepting responsibility for the damage it has done, and continues to do, to our people? Well, my long experience suggests there are several different paths we might take, each with their own opportunities and temptations. I want to spend a little time describing them now, because I believe it is crucially important that we engage with the church in the full light of the new day that Christ has brought with him from the dead. Every possible pathway needs to be examined carefully under the aegis of that light if we are to avoid the traps, the dead-ends, and the many false trails that bedevil the enterprise of genuine reconciliation.

1. The way of denial

The first path we might choose to take is that of denial. For our people, denial involves minimising your 'blackness' and pretending that you are a 'white' person, if only an 'honorary' white person, because doing so makes life a lot less complicated. This is a particularly easy path to take for those of us who (according the racist narrative of the coloniser) 'look' white, or who grew up in the south-east of the continent where the impact of colonialism was at its most severe. Here the policies of government for 150 years were explicitly designed to 'breed out the blackness' by removing children from their land, their parents, their siblings and all the sources of traditional language and culture. Resisting these policies was almost impossible and, if you were caught doing so, the punishments could range from having your mouth washed out with soap (for speaking in language) and being beaten or chained up in solitary confinement (for disobeying an instruction) to being hanged (for armed resistance). For 150 years, those of us who grew up in the south-east have been told that we are not Aboriginal and the sooner we got that notion out of our heads the better things would go for us. So too, for those of us who grew up in the church. The vast majority of our fellow Christians were taught by parents and teachers that there are no Aboriginal people left in this part of the country, that we all 'died out' because our bodies had no resistance to European diseases, or because we were too stupid to adapt to the civilizing influence of European society. When most of your fellow-worshippers live in that kind of imaginative universe, life is more straight-forward if you, quite simply, keep your Indigeneity hidden away in the most secret compartment of your heart!

At least, that is what the coloniser would like you to think. Actually, there are few worse things than pretending you are something you are not. Doing so can set up such a violent conflict in your personhood that it will eventually eat away all your joy in life. It will make you sick, it may even take your life. And because most of our people suffer from the effects of intergenerational trauma—even if we have never experienced the worst of the colonising practices ourselves, personally—we are highly susceptible to a whole range of chronic health conditions, especially those that effect the mind and the heart. I know from long personal experience that the *one thing* that has the power to take away my voice, my joy, my reason for getting out of bed in the morning, is being told I don't exist and coming to believe that lie. So, denying who you are is no path to salvation. It is the opposite: it is the path to hell and all its furies. So, when the church pressures you to be an invisible honorary white, resist, resist, resist! Resist as though your life depends on it. Because it probably does.

2. The way of righteous anger and soul-crippling despair

This is a path I know intimately, as intimately as the contours of the sacred mountain that dominated the southern horizon in my home town. It is the way most taken by many of our most visible warriors and activists. And it is easy to see why. Anger for the sake of a worthy cause, the cause of justice, makes you feel righteous and it makes you feel powerful. And—God knows!—most of our people do not often feel such things these days! Instead, under the crushing weight of the colonial legacy, many of us actually feel ashamed of who we are: primitive people, dirty people, defeated people who have been consigned to the dust-bin of history (a history written by white people). We have so internalised the colonial version of who we are, and what we are worth, that we consign ourselves to a kind of existential smallness, taking up as little space in the world as possible and seeking, constantly, to placate our betters and accede to their wishes for fear of becoming not only small but nothing at all.

By contrast, the path of righteous anger has proven, time and time again, to swell the chest of the Aboriginal or Torres Strait Islander warrior and give us the power to contest the dominant position of the coloniser and call the colonial way of rendering the world into question. For those of us who are Christians, we can legitimately invoke the example of Christ himself as our model. Was Christ ever more angry than when he gave the Jewish leaders a tongue-lashing in Matthew chapter 23? I think not. Here is a sample of what he had to say:

> Woe to you, scribes and Pharisees, hypocrites! For you lock people out of the kingdom of heaven. For you do not go in yourselves, and when others are going in, you stop them. Woe to you, scribes and Pharisees, hypocrites! For you cross sea and land to make a single convert, and you make the new convert twice as much a child of hell as yourselves . . .
>
> Woe to you, scribes and Pharisees, hypocrites! For you tithe mint, dill, and cummin, and have neglected the weightier matters of the law: justice and mercy and faith. It is these you ought to have practised without neglecting the others. You blind guides! You strain out a gnat but swallow a camel!

> Woe to you, scribes and Pharisees, hypocrites! For you clean the outside of the cup and of the plate, but inside they are full of greed and self-indulgence. You blind Pharisee! First clean the inside of the cup, so that the outside also may become clean.
>
> Woe to you, scribes and Pharisees, hypocrites! For you are like whitewashed tombs, which on the outside look beautiful, but inside they are full of the bones of the dead and of all kinds of filth. So you also on the outside look righteous to others, but inside you are full of hypocrisy and lawlessness.
>
> Woe to you, scribes and Pharisees, hypocrites! For you build the tombs of the prophets and decorate the graves of the righteous, and you say, "If we had lived in the days of our ancestors, we would not have taken part with them in shedding the blood of the prophets." Thus you testify against yourselves that you are descendants of those who murdered the prophets. Fill up, then, the measure of your ancestors. You snakes, you brood of vipers! How can you escape being sentenced to hell? Therefore I send you prophets, sages, and scribes, some of whom you will kill and crucify, and some you will flog in your synagogues and pursue from town to town, so that upon you may come all the righteous blood shed on earth, from the blood of righteous Abel to the blood of Zechariah son of Barachiah, whom you murdered between the sanctuary and the altar.

I remember when I read this passage as a teenager, along with its companion passages in Luke 11:37–53 and Mark 11:12–19, I felt my chest swell. For here I learned of a God who was as angry as I was with those who exploited and used the poor and the vulnerable to feather their own nests and enhance their wealth and prestige in the world. And that anger filled me with the energy and the desire to fight for a better world, for a commonwealth in which the poor were lifted up and the corrupt rulers were brought to their knees (*cf* the *Magnificat* in Lk 1:46–55). And fight I did, mainly through the use of my pen and my lips, for God had given me the 'gift of the gab', as the Irish say. So, anger is good. It is full of energy. It is the fuel from which the fires of revolutionary justice can be lit.

However, there is a shadow side to anger. Psychologically, because anger burns, it also consumes one's energy very quickly. The person who stays angry will oftentimes burn themselves out fast, by which time the anger will have transformed into something else: despair, or *accidie*, the 'noon-day demon' of depression described by the desert fathers and mothers of Egypt. This rather negative process of transformation can often reveal a form of self-loathing. For as one's powers begin to wane, as the energy for the righteous fight begins to drain away, the angry warrior often begins to accuse his or herself of precisely the kind of unrighteousness she or he is seeking to expose and change. 'If I, myself, cannot stay the course until the goal is met, the prize is won, then perhaps I am no better than the careless elites who create and maintain the systems of exploitation. Perhaps, in the end, I care only for myself and not for the kinspeople who need me.' It is, of course, the demon who accuses. It is the sin within, as St Paul would say. But when you are exhausted because you are a young warrior who has not yet learned the value of prayer and sabbath-rest as sources of replenishment, it is the demon who very often wins the day, or the week, or even the year. I have had a long battle with the demon depression—*dysthymia*, as the medics call it—and have spent not months but years under its sway. In the end, the only way I have found to regain some perspective is twofold: (1) to develop a strong discipline of daily prayer in which I was able to hear, again, that the God of Jesus Christ loved me unconditionally and had not yet done with me; and (2) to make a twice-yearly pilgrimage back to my island home to hear there the ancestral voices of encouragement and reassurance that speak to my people from the land and the sea.

Anger is seductive because it is full of energy. But it can also make you drunk with unrealistic fantasies about your own strength, skill and prowess in the cause. In my experience, the crash back to earth is humbling in the best possible way. It reminds you, as the apostle taught, that the most excellent way is neither prophecy nor searing insight, but love (1 Corinthians 13). Without a palpable experience of the forgiving, empowering, love of God and of other people, we can none of us be whom we are called to be. Without a visceral sense of walking the way to justice in the company of others, who support us as much as we support them, reconciliation will remain just a fool's fantasy. Love forgives. Love binds up our wounds. Love picks us up and trains us in a righteousness that empowers us to take just one more step along the road to justice for our people.

3. The way of the loving witness to truth

We are at the heart of my reflections now, dear kin. I want to share with you now a description of the path I believe all of us must walk if we are to 'give peace a chance' not only in the church, but in Australian life as a whole.

The writer to the Ephesians had a dream about what a mature, grown-up, church might look like:

> Then we will no longer be infants, tossed back and forth by the waves, and blown here and there by every wind of teaching and by the cunning and craftiness of men in their deceitful scheming. Instead, speaking the truth in love, we will in all things grow up into him who is the Head, that is, Christ. From him the whole body, joined and held together by every supporting ligament, grows and builds itself up in love, as each part does its work (4:14–16).

If we are to grow up into Christ, who is God's *shalom*, the one in whom the dividing principles of hostility and enmity are put to death (2:14–18), then we are called to speak 'truth' to each other; but we should do so 'in love'. What does this mean for us as First Peoples? It means, first, that we should never abandon the truth of what we have experienced and known in our history and in our own bodies. In the light of the gospel, it is plain that the country given us by God has been stolen from us at the point of a gun; that our communities and cultures have been raped and torn asunder with the approval and willing participation of the churches; that the churches continue to favour 'soft' approaches to reconciliation over more substantial acts of repentance, restitution and amendment of life. These truths we carry in our bodies as scars, scars which mirror and point to the very scars of Christ, and we should never waver from a clear presentation of this scarified truth in conversation with our fellow Christians, whether formal or informal.

Now, to many of you that may seem obvious. Yet, the history of our dealings with the churches would suggest that all too often we put such truths aside because we are worried that the recognition we are already given by the church might dry up and disappear. As I've said already, too often we succumb to a 'mission' mentality, continually placating the boss or mission-manager so that he will not punish us.

By doing so, we not only infantilise ourselves, but we also allow the churches to be become comfortable with the falsely heroic stories they tell about themselves in relation to our people. We therefore become aiders and abettors in such falsehoods, unwitting agents of the 'father of lies' (Jn 8:44) who ultimately contribute to the ongoing colonisation of our lands, imaginations and bodies. I'm not sure I can put it any more plainly than that.

And yet, our commitment to the truth of our experience, a truth made plain in the light of the Christian gospel, must not prevent us from speaking such truth 'in love'. If we are Christians, and not simply warriors who are scrapping with each other to gain power for power's sake, we must take seriously the injunction to 'love your neighbour as you love yourself' (Mark 21.31). For Christians, you see, love has a content. It is not a word that can be conveniently filled with any meaning that suits us at the time. Love is not a Hollywood movie! Love, rather, is the way God deals with us in Christ. It is that kenotic (self-emptying) kind of love that puts itself on the line so that another may live and grow and flourish. It is the love that is willing even to die that another might grow up into the truth of whom God has called them to be.

Now, for us as First People's—as the people who, in this country, are least loved—I want to suggest that the call to love takes a particular shape. And that is the shape suggested by the story of the woman who approaches Jesus in chapter 15 of Matthew's gospel:

> Jesus left that place and went away to the district of Tyre and Sidon. Just then a Canaanite woman from that region came out and started shouting, 'Have mercy on me, Lord, Son of David; my daughter is tormented by a demon.' But he did not answer her at all. And his disciples came and urged him, saying, 'Send her away, for she keeps shouting after us.' He answered, 'I was sent only to the lost sheep of the house of Israel.' But she came and knelt before him, saying, 'Lord, help me.' He answered, 'It is not fair to take the children's food and throw it to the dogs.' She said, 'Yes, Lord, yet even the dogs eat the crumbs that fall from their masters' table.' Then Jesus answered her, 'Woman, great is your faith! Let it be done for you as you wish.' And her daughter was healed instantly (15:21-28).

The woman is a Canaanite, one of the original inhabitants of Palestine. Since the Canaanites, in the time of Jesus, are a thoroughly colonised people, the demon who afflicts her daughter is probably a lot like the demons that afflict our people: poverty, illness, self-loathing, grief. When Jesus does not respond to her call for help—most probably because of an internal debate between what love requires and what Jewish custom would allow—she persists; she keeps demanding his attention. But she does so in a way that accords him respect, for she names him 'Lord, Son of David', at the very least a recognition that he is a person whose power and authority are legitimate. Because she persists, and despite his disciple's protestations that she ought to be sent away, Jesus eventually tells her that he was 'sent only to the lost sheep of the house of Israel' of which she, of course, was not a member. Jesus then says, 'It is not right to take the children's bread and give it to their dogs'. Jewish custom, it seems, had won out over the requirements of love. End of story. But the Canaanite woman will not allow the story to end there. Because she loves her daughter so much that she is willing to risk the ire of her 'betters', and because she has an unshakable belief that the love of God is actually more generous than Jewish racism will allow, she proposes an alternative theological argument: 'Yes Lord, but even the dogs eat the crumbs that fall from their master's tables'. In the context of *this* story, in the face of a racism that is *this self-righteous,* to propose that the rabbi might actually be wrong in his assumption that she is undeserving of his attention is not only courageous but also deeply faithful to her own experience of God. Clearly her experience with God has taught her something that Jesus himself had not yet learned: that God's love extends even to those beyond one's own tribe; that God loves the neighbour who belongs to another tribe as much as he loves the neighbour who belongs to one's own. Radical stuff in the first century! And yet, as we have seen, even the 'enlightened' Christians of modern liberal societies such as ours continue to struggle with its implications.

The response of Jesus is decisive. After resuming the internal debate, he finally concludes that she is right: 'Woman, you have great faith! Your request is granted'. To be named a person of 'great' faith by Jesus is actually very rare in the gospel of Matthew. In fact, great faith is never once ascribed to the children of Abraham. It is reserved only for the Canaanite woman and the Roman centurion of Capernaum (cf. 8:10). It is clear, also, that Jesus learns something very important through this encounter, for immediately afterwards he decides to continue his mission of preaching, healing and exorcism with an extended stay in the region of Tyre and Sidon, a decidedly multicultural province of the Roman world. Clearly Jesus was teachable in a way that many modern church leaders are not!

Dear First Nations kin, let us learn from the actions of the Canaanite woman. Let us persist in seeking mercy, help, and justice from the churches to which we belong, recognising always that the churches are not as perfect in learning their mission as Jesus was. And let us do so because we are motivated by love—for our suffering First Nations kin, certainly—but also for the settler peoples of our churches, who continue to participate in our oppression. As the Baptist scholar Athol Gill taught me a long time ago, the good news for the oppressor is that they need no longer be oppressors! We should love our enemies, our oppressors, by praying for them; but also by seeking to liberate them from the lies in which they have become so tragically entangled. For, in the end, the oppressor is as much a victim of their oppression as the people they seek to oppress. It was not until Jesus had been released from his ethno-centric racism that he was able to extend his mission of mercy to everyone. It was not until the Canaanite woman had shared with him her faith in a God who loved all tribes that Jesus was able to start a movement which crossed ethnic boundaries with a truly universal gospel of reconciliation. So too, in our conversations with the churches to which we belong, let us strongly insist that only the truth is able to set us free, *all of us,* First and settler peoples together. And let us do so because of love.

Postscript
A Christian Eucharist for Gondwana[1]

This rite seeks to draw on the Australian landscape and the experience of First Nations people with God as much as on the Anglo-catholic tradition.[2] It seeks to create a conversation between the two that will open up new regions of imagination in all of us concerning God, neighbour, and our shared habitation in Australia.

This rite does not pretend to be comprehensive, suitable for all times and places. It seeks only to suggest and provoke more local, contextually aware, iterations. I have sought to be economical with words, preferring that silence and movement be embraced as dimensions of worship that are equally significant.

The rite assumes that the congregation will gather in something of a circle or semi-circle. The altar table is placed at the centre of the circle. The font is placed at the point of entry to the circle, and the lectern immediately opposite. The processions at the beginning, middle, and end of the rite will, therefore, be necessarily circular in nature.[3]

1. *Gondwana* is a neologism derived from central Indian Sanskrit, originally referring to the forests inhabited by the Gond people. Austrian scientist Eduard Suess used it to name the southern supercontinent out of which Australia originally emerged.
2. In this instance, I am drawing liberally from 'The Holy Communion Second Order' in *A Prayer Book for Australia* (Sydney: Broughton Publishing, 1995). Unless otherwise cited, departures from the text are the work of the current author.
3. I owe this sense of space to my time as an associate pastor at the South Yarra Community Baptist Church in Melbourne. It was a community which allowed me, in consultation with Nathan Nettleton, the senior pastor, to experiment with worship in a way I never been able to do so before.

GATHERING IN GOD'S NAME

PROCESSIONAL HYMN

The people stand. The presider enters during the hymn, following a procession that may include a crucifix, a gospel book or bible, and icons of significant local saints or ancestors. Each is put in its place. A thurifer may cense the holy people and the holy things with incense inspired by native aromas.

When the hymn is finished, the presider greets the people:

Blessed be God, Father, Son and Holy Spirit.
Blessed be God's country, now and for ever.

The Lord be with you.
And also with you.

The people are welcomed to worship and given a brief introduction to the themes of the day.

This, or a seasonal sentence may be used to call the people to worship:

'The earth is God's, and everything in it,
the cosmos and all who find their home therein;
for God founded it upon the oceans
and caused it to grow in the midst of the waters'.

Psalm 24:1-2

This or a seasonal prayer of invocation follows:

Let us pray.

O God of our ancestors, God who speaks with us through the weave of our dreaming; God of Israel, who rescued your people from slavery in Egypt,
come now to comfort your people.

A brief silence may be kept.

O God our Wisdom, you who sang the ancient walkways into being; Jesus our brother, who sings us along the ancient pathways, through death and despair to a land flowing with nectar and with honey,

come now to save your people.

A brief silence may be kept.

O God the Spirit, breath of life and holy fire;
God of gracious abundance, who fills all that is alive with both joy and holy purpose,
come now to renew your people.

A brief silence may be kept before the singing of the *Gloria in excelsis* or another song of praise to the Holy Trinity.
This collect, or the collect of the day is prayed:

Blessed God, Ancient Spirit of Gondwana,
you are the one in whom we live and move and have our being,
you are the one who nurtures and feeds us
with the pure nectar of our ancient faith.
Come now, Blessed One, gather us together in a spirit of hospitality,
that we may welcome your own wisdom in each other's wisdom,
and hear your own voice in each other's voices.
Help us to patiently wait for the word of liberation,
that our hurts may be indeed be healed
and our work for others hallowed.
Help us to do so after the example of Jesus our Lord,
he who lives and reigns with you in the unity of the Holy Spirit,
one God for ever and ever. **Amen.**

THE MINISTRY OF THE WORD

The congregation is seated as the readers take their place at the lectern. Before reading, each acknowledges the holy book with a bow.
The first lection is introduced with the following dialogue:

A reading from the book of . . . . , chapter . . . , beginning at verse . . .
Let us listen for the word of God.

When the lection is concluded, the reader says:

The word of the Lord.
Thanks be to God.

The Psalm of the day is said or sung either responsively or antiphonally, with the guidance of a cantor.

The second lection is introduced with the following dialogue:

A reading from the book of . . . . , chapter . . . , beginning at verse . . .
Let us listen for the word of God.

When the lection is concluded, the reader says:

The word of the Lord.
Thanks be to God.

The people stand. The gospel book is processed to either the font or the Lord's table (if these are within the circle of the gathered community), or else a central point in the midst of the people. An anthem may be sung as this happens. The gospel is introduced with this dialogue:

The Lord be with you.
And also with you.

A reading from the holy gospel according to St . . . , chapter . . . , beginning at verse . . .
Glory to you, Lord Jesus Christ.

When the gospel is concluded, the reader holds the holy book aloft and says:

The Gospel of the Lord.
Praise to you, Lord Jesus Christ.

The holy book is processed back to its usual place.
The congregation is seated.

A homily on the texts of the day is then preached, followed by several minutes of silent meditation.

The presider then introduces this, or another, affirmation of faith:

Let us stand to affirm the faith of the church.

We believe in God,
who created the world in love,
who led the First Peoples to this land,
who rescued Israel from slavery in Egypt,
who sent the ancestors and the prophets to judge and to bless,
who returns the exiles to their home,
whom Jesus called his Father.

We believe in Jesus Christ,
born of Mary, born under law,
Son of David and Son of God,
proclaimer of God's peace with justice,
healer and exorcist,
tortured and crucified by evil men,
sacrament of God's love,
risen to reconcile all the world,
coming again to make the world new.

We believe in the Holy Spirit,
whose breath gave life to creation,
who speaks through ancestors and prophets,
who is the love between the Father and the Son,
who came upon Jesus at his baptism,
who gives birth to the church, Christ's body,
who pours out gifts for the ministry of love,
who works night and day to renew all that is alive.

We believe in God, the Father, the Son and the Holy Spirit.
Amen!

THE PRAYERS OF THE PEOPLE

The presider says:

Let us pray for the church and for the world,
that God may change our hearts of stone to hearts that can feel.

Another minister then continues.

In peace, let us pray to the Lord saying:
Lord, hear us:
Lord, hear our prayer.

Prayers are offered for the church and for the world, according to local custom.
Following the formal payers, a time of unguided prayer may follow. Prayer stations may be visited, where (for example) candles are lit or stones placed in water, each a sign of someone's prayer. Quiet music may accompany this time.

The prayers are concluded with this prayer or another, based on the lections of the day:

O great God of Gondwana,
who keeps your *makarrata* of love with all who love and obey you;[4]
may your eyes and ears be open to the cries of your servants.
Suggested by Nehemiah 1:5-6

Hear our prayers, that the world may be healed.
Hear our prayers, that the world may be healed.

LITURGY OF THE TABLE

CONFESSION OR LAMENT

The prayers are introduced with this sentence, or another taken from the lections of the day:

'If we claim to be without sin, we lie to ourselves and the truth is far from us. If we own up to our sins, God is faithful and just; God will forgive our sins and cleanse every dirty stain.'
1 John 1:8-9

In a moment of silent prayer, let us then lament/confess our sins in penitence and faith.

Silence is kept.

4. *Makarrata* is a word in the Yolngu language meaning a coming together after a struggle, facing the facts of wrongs and living again in peace. Yolgnu country is in north-east Arnhem Land in the Northern Territory.

A prayer of either (A) Lament or (B) Confession is then said. Either may be replaced by a seasonal variation.

(A) Lament in three voices

Voice 1:
God of love, creator of this ancient land,
We are a nation divided in many ways:
  city against country
  rich against poor
  man against woman
  industry against environment.
Today we gather to name, with heavy hearts,
the longstanding hurts which divide First and settler Australians.

Voice 2:
We lament the grief and heartache caused by
the invasion of this continent by Europeans,
the taking of Aboriginal and Torres Strait Islander territories without permission,
the rape and torture of First Nations women, men and children,
the policy of assimilation and the dislocation of Indigenous families.
Lord of life, encourage all Australians to dream and live for a new vision:
help us to imagine a land in which all may share in the gospel
values of justice, peace and harmony with our environment.

Voice 3:
Mysterious God, creator of life and bearer of pain,
we pray earnestly this day for reconciliation between
First and settler Australians.
Change our hearts of stone into hearts that feel;
transform our hollow words into works of peace and compassion.
Give us a deep respect and care for one another,
that we may listen to each other's stories without fear or prejudice.
Help us to walk and talk a renewed vision for Australia;
and give us the courage to see it through.
Ancient Spirit of Gondwana,
come upon your people gathered here.
Bless and keep us in the changes we make this day.
Amen.

(B) Confession

In the beginning when the earth was made,
God brought forth life and light from the watery depths.
And God saw that it was good.
But look what we have done!
In the clouds of industry the light is hidden;
and life itself struggles for breath amidst the stench of human greed.
(sung): **Kyrie eleison . . .**

In the beginning when the earth was made,
the land emerged and burst forth with vegetation.
And God saw that it was good.
But look what we have done!
With 'green revolutions' and the love of money
we've endangered the variety on which all life depends.
(sung): **Christe eleison . . .**

In the beginning when the earth was made,
the sea was filled with fish, and the sky with birds,
and the land with creatures from God's secret purpose.
And God saw that it was good.
But look what we have done!
Our brother the Thylacine and our sister the Pig-footed Bandicoot
wander the bush no more.
(sung): **Kyrie eleison . . .**

This or another seasonal absolution follows:

Listen to what God says:
'A shoot shall come out from the stump of Jesse,
and a branch shall grow out of his roots.
He shall not judge by rumour or by so-called 'common sense'.
With righteousness he shall judge for the little ones,
with justice he shall decide for the one most vulnerable.
The dingo shall live with the kangaroo,
the calf and the croc and the emu together;
and a little child shall look out for them.

Suggested by Isaiah 11:1, 3, 4, 6

Therefore, Christ has this word of grace
for all who lament their complicity with all that is wrong in the world,

who come to God with a broken and contrite spirit:
'Your sins are forgiven.'
Thanks be to God!

At Easter, especially, the congregation may be asperged three times with baptismal water as the presider says:

In Christ you died to sin once and for all.
Always remember that you are baptised and give thanks to God.
If you are not baptised, know that Christ calls you to the waters,
to die, and be buried, and to rise with him.

The congregation may respond:

Alleluia! Praise the Lord!

THE GREETING OF PEACE

This, or a sentence taken from the lections of the day, introduces the greeting of peace:

Hear the word of John the Evangelist:
'God did not send the son into the world to condemn the world, but that the world might be saved through him.'

John 3:17

The congregation stands.

Christ has reconciled us to God in one body by the cross.
We meet in his name and share his peace.
The peace of the Lord be always with you.
And also with you.

A sign of peace is shared.

OFFERTORY HYMN

During the hymn, the gifts are brought to the Lord's table. The table is prepared and the ablutions made. The holy people and the holy things may be censed once more.

Blessed are you Lord, God of all creation.
Through your goodness we have these gifts to share.
Fruit of the earth and work of human hands,
they will become, for us, the body and blood of Christ.
Blessed be God for ever.

Blessed are you Lord, God of all creation.
Through your goodness we have this food and this money to share.
Fruit of the earth and produce from our labour,
they will become signs of your love for all who are poor or downtrodden.
Blessed be God for ever.

The people stand.

The presider begins the Great Prayer.

The Lord be with you.
And also with you.
Lift up your hearts.
We lift them to the Lord.
Let us give thanks to the Lord our God.
It is right to give our thanks and praise.

God we praise you because in the beginning you created a garden and asked us to share with you in the joy of making it fruitful. In company with our ancestors, you provided earth, sun, grain and water, everything we needed to live and work with joy. But we got greedy. Instead of sharing what we produced with you, we decided to keep it all for ourselves. So you sent your Old People, the custodians and prophets, to call us back to the joy of sharing together in covenant relationship. But we would not listen, adding torture and murder to our sins. In time you sent your Son, but we killed him also. That was when darkness descended on the world. That was when joy took its flight.

We praise you God that you did not abandon us to our darkness and greed. As Christ rose from his grave to fill the whole world with light, we saw the strength of your love. Strong and constant, you promised that the earth will again bear the fruit of joy for everyone who turns from their greed to embrace Christ's loving-kindness. We praise you, God, that our greed will never be strong enough to exhaust your infinite generosity.

Therefore, with angels and saints,
and with the ancestors who envelop us in earth, sea and sky,
we sing the hymn of unending praise:

Holy, holy, holy Lord,
God of power and might.
Heaven and earth are full of your glory.
Hosanna in the highest.
Blessed is he who comes in the name of the Lord.
Hosanna in the highest.

Blessed are you, God of life, and blessed is the Holy One you sent to save us. In our affliction, Christ drew near to renew his people in a spirit of mercy, justice and peace. He became our sister Garrangabumarri (pelican) who, when times are desperate, feeds her nestlings with her very own blood.[5] Christ was not afraid to make *makarrata* with us, to touch and embrace us in the night of our sin with a message of generosity and care, that we might all find courage to share your bounty once more. For this we shall praise and glorify you for ever.

We recall how, on the night in which he was betrayed, Jesus took bread, gave thanks, and shared it with his friends saying: 'This is my body, given for you. Whenever you eat it, remember me.'

In the same way after they had eaten he took a cup of wine and, again giving thanks, he bid them drink: 'This is my blood,' he said. 'I shed it for you to make a new covenant with God. Whenever you drink of it, remember me. I tell you the truth, I shall not again drink the fruit of the vine until I share it with you in the kingdom of God.'

An assistant minister may say:

Therefore, here in this place, we celebrate the death by which God makes us alive:

Christ has died;
Christ is risen;
Christ will come again.

5. *Garrangabumarri* is a Tharawal word for 'Pelican'. Tharawal country spreads from the south of Sydney Harbour, through Georges River, Botany Bay, Port Hacking, throughout the Illawarra Escarpment, and across areas now known as the Macarthur, Southern Highlands, and Illawarra regions, as far south as the Shoalhaven River.

Come Holy Spirit, come. Make of this bread Christ's body. Make of the wine his blood. As we share the meal together, make us one with Christ, one with each other, and one in the ministry we share as his body, broken that our country might be made whole.

Through Christ, with Christ, and in Christ, all creation sings your praise, holy Father:

Blessing and honour and glory and power
are yours for ever and ever. Amen.

An assistant minister says:

Let us pray together the prayer that Jesus taught us.

Our Father in heaven,
hallowed be your name,
your kingdom come,
your will be done,
on earth as in heaven.
Give us today our daily bread.
Forgive us our sins
as we forgive those who sin against us.
Save us from the time of trial
and deliver us from evil.
For the kingdom, the power, and the glory are yours
now and for ever. Amen.

FRACTION AND COMMUNION

The people are seated.
The presider breaks the bread in full view of the people, saying:

We break this bread to share in the body of Christ.
We who are many are one body,
for we all share in the one bread.

As the bread is prepared, the *agnus dei* is said or sung:

Jesus, lamb of God,
have mercy on us.
Jesus, bearer of our sins,
have mercy on us.

Jesus, redeemer of the world,
grant us your peace.

The presider invites the congregation to communion with these or other suitable words:

This is the feast of the baptised, those who struggle with God and find that God is love. So, come to this meal not because you are strong but because you are fragile. Come not because of any virtue you may possess but because you trust in Christ's goodness. Come because you love the Lord a little and would like to love him more.

The gifts of God for the people of God.
Let us receive who we are, let us become what we receive:
The body of Christ.[6]

The people commune according to local custom.

THE SENDING OUT OF GOD'S PEOPLE

The people stand and the presider says this or another exhortation to mission:

Don't be afraid, God's love is stronger than your fear. Don't be afraid. God has promised you hope and a future. So let go of your concerns, and let God in. Rise up on the wings of Bunjil. Then your faith will shine like the sun in the boorondara of our world.[7]

The congregation is then blessed in the name of the Holy Trinity:

God's blessing be upon you always—that of the Father, the Son and Holy Spirit.

An assistant minister then dismisses the people, saying:

6. This responsorial comes from 'The Service of the Lord's Day: Second Service' in *Uniting in Worship 2*, (Sydney: Uniting Church Press, 2005).
7. *Bunjil* is the eagle-ancestor in Kulin dreaming stories. *Boorondara* in a Woi Wurrung word from the Kulin people in Melbourne. It means, roughly: darkness, shade or nighttime.

Go in peace to love and serve the Lord.
In the name of Christ. Amen.

RECESSIONAL HYMN

During the hymn, the holy things are processed from the worship space. The people remain standing until the presider has departed.

Further Resources for use with this Eucharist

INVOCATION AND PRAISE

Advent

O blessed Wisdom,
coming towards us on the breath of God,
seeping into every crack and corner of the world
with strength and gentleness to order everything just right:
Come now and show us the way to health and wholeness.
Come Lord, come quickly.

O blessed Adonai
hope of God's people,
you made yourself known to Moses in a burning bush,
and let him in on life's best secrets:
Come now, take us into your confidence as well.
Come Lord, come quickly.

O blessed Root of Jesse,
budding from a dead branch as a sign of hope for everyone;
the leaders of the world will stand in amazement at you,
and all their people as well:
Come quickly to deliver us from the rottenness of our politics.
Come Lord, come quickly.

O blessed Key of David,
true Pastor of all God's people,
you open doors that no-one can close,
and close doors that no-one can open:
Come now to set the prisoners free,
all those who live in darkness and despair.
Come Lord, come quickly.

O Radiant Dawn,
glory and beauty of God's own face,
eternal Sun of justice and peace:
Come now to shine for everyone
who lives in the shadow of death.
Come Lord, come quickly.

O blessed Shepherd of all the world,
desire of every people and nation,
you are the heartbeat of our fragile humanity:
Come now to save us,
we whom you formed from the dust of the earth.
Come Lord, come quickly.

O blessed Emmanuel,
rightful ruler and giver of the secrets of life,
desire of every heart and saviour of the world:
Come now to make us your children,
for you are our God, the Lord of all.
Come Lord, come quickly.

Inspired by the traditional 'O' antiphons of Advent

Christmas

In the beginning was the Word:
the Word was with God and was the same as God.
Glory to God in the highest!

The Word became a human being and lived among us:
Jesus, who is close to the Father's heart, has made God known.
Glory to God in the highest!

In Jesus is life, and that life is the light of all people:
the light shines in the darkness, and the darkness has not overcome it.
Glory to God in the highest,
and peace to God's people on earth!

Based on John 1:1, 14, 4 and Luke 2:14

Epiphany

Your love, O Lord, reaches to the heavens,
your faithfulness is as big as the desert sky.
Your justice is as firm and sure as Uluru.
To you we, and all living things, owe our very existence.

You send out your Spirit and we are created.
You take your Spirit away, and we are no more.
Your love for us is immeasurable, beyond any price to buy.
You give your love freely.
Both rich and poor find refuge in the shadow of your wings.
They feast on the abundance of your household,
and drink from your river of delight.
In your light, are we enlightened and find the truth of things.
Only in your light, do we see and hear from is really important.
And so we praise you God – Father, Son and Holy Spirit.
All glory is yours, for ever and ever. Amen.

Baptism of Jesus

God of wonders,
in the beginning your Spirit hovered over the watery void,
giving life to nothingness and form to chaos.
Come, Holy Spirit;
breathe your life into our lacklustre lives.

At the exodus of your people from slavery, your Spirit blew across the waters of the red sea; through those watery depths a path was made to freedom.
Come, Holy Spirit;
breathe your freedom into our many captivities.

At the baptism of Jesus your Spirit came from on high to call him your Son and to make of his life, his words and his deeds, a sacrament of salvation.
Come, Holy Spirit;
breathe your purpose into our hesitating and uncertain flesh.

The Baptism of Jesus

Lord of love
at his baptism Jesus faced our traditional fear of death by water.

Water,
the huge seas that can snaps boats in two as though they were matches, and devastate coastal villages in a minute flat.
Water,
the pool or the river where so many drown,
a grey maelstrom where breath and spirit are starved.

Water,
the dwelling-place of sea-monsters, sirens, and alien creatures,
a place of deep darkness where nothing is safe.

In the waters Jesus drowned indeed, putting his fears to death.
But then you raised him, called him your own, and gave him a mission:
to call everyone to die to themselves as he did,
so that you can raise them to breathe the air of freedom.

Loving Lord,
as we today recall the story of when Christ was baptised,
give us power enough to live out our own baptism:
give us courage to die to everything that keeps us in chains,
and be reborn to the mission of love you have given us.

Transfiguration

God of Moses and Elijah, God of the whirlwind and of fire:
In you alone can we find our peace. Come now, give us a double-portion of your Spirit, that we may speak and do as your prophets speak and do.
Come, God of the whirlwind, come.

Jesus our Teacher, brother and friend:
In you alone we hear a word that liberates. Come now, transfigure our lifeless bodies that we, also, may show forth the glory of God's indwelling love.
Come, Christ our light, come.

Spirit most holy, breath of God and water of life:
In you alone may we experience all the fullness of life. Come now, make of these faces of ours the very face of Christ, a treasure hidden in jars of clay, that the world may see in us the loving gaze of God.
Come, Spirit most holy, come.

In all *we* do this day, most glorious God, may *your* work be done first of all. Make of our words *your* Word. Make of our signs *your* Sign. Make of our hearts *your* heart. Come now, fill your people to overflowing with all that is good, and beautiful and true.
Glory be to you, God most holy. Glory be.

Lent

All glory is yours, God of Israel!
Your beauty is alive in all of creation, strong and constant even where your children have sought to smear or crush your beautiful imprint.
Glory be to the God of Israel!
Glory be to the God of Israel!

All glory is yours, Christ our brother!
You came amongst us as the face, feet and hands of divine love, reaching out to the heal and exorcise your enslaved people.
Glory be to Christ our brother!
Glory be to Christ our brother!

All glory is yours, Spirit most holy! You are the promise that we are never left forsaken but chosen, empowered, inpired even, to weave the pattern of Christ's love into the fabric of our world. Glory be to the Spirit most Holy!
Glory be to the Spirit most Holy!

Today you have gathered us for worship, O God.
So visit us now with your mercy, your courage, and your wisdom,
that we may leave this place a nourished and refreshed people,
ready to do your bidding amongst friends and enemies alike. **Amen.**

Lent

Blessed are you, God of love,
the leader of your people, Israel.
You go before us: a pillar of cloud by day,
and a pillar of fire by night.
During these forty days you lead us into the desert of repentance,
that by this pilgrimage we may turn, again, to your ways.
We hear you call us to forsake our selfish living
and turn, again, to Christ,
that you may embrace and welcome us home
from the far country of our wandering.
You lead us along the path of discipleship
and we are marked with the scars of your cross.
Be with us, Lord, through the dark of the night,
for without your light, we shall lose the way.[8]

8. Adapted from *Uniting in Worship: People's Book* (Sydney: Uniting Church Press, 1988), p. 155.

Lent

God our Father, you made human beings in your image and breathed into us the breath of life:

Come now to complete your holy work.

Jesus, friend and brother,
you promised a new birth for all who turn to you in faith:

Come, give us your courage to believe in God's promise.

Spirit most Holy, midwife of God and water of life:

Come now to birth the kingdom of God in our midst.

Lent

Creator God, liberator of slaves and provider of all good things:

with our bodies we worship you.

Jesus Christ, friend of sinners and bringer of joy:

with our voices we sing your praise.

Spirit most Holy, water of life to quench our thirsty souls:

with mind and spirit we adore you.

Lent

God our Father and Mother, when we are lost, you come looking for us in the valleys of our hopelessness.

God of all mercy, we praise you.

Jesus, when we have resigned ourselves to the inevitable, you surprise us with impossible deeds,

God of all hope, we worship you.

Spirit most Holy, when the life within us seems to have ebbed away forever, you come to make 'forever' but an instant in time.

God of resurrection, we adore you.

Lent

God of Noah, we praise you. Through water you destroyed the earth and through water you renewed it. Come now to renew us in the covenant of baptism, that we who have died with Christ may evermore live with him in all the joy of the children of God.

God of Noah, we praise you.
God of Noah, we praise you.

Jesus, our brother, we praise you. Through water and through wilderness you put aside all those common callings to tribe and country and chose, instead, the vocation your father had chosen for you: to suffer the life of a Son who cries 'repent, for the kingdom of God is near!'

Jesus, our brother, we praise you.

Jesus, our brother, we praise you.

Spirit most holy, we praise you. Like a dove you descended on Jesus at his baptism. Like a wild willy-wind you drove him into the wilderness to be tempted by Satan. Come to us now, with all your persuasive power and compassion, that we who would share in Christ's resurrection would also be willing to share in his cross. Purge us, Holy Spirit, of all that would hold us back from the free-fall of faith. Wash us clean that we might embrace all that is good, and glorious, and true.

Spirit most holy, we praise you.

Spirit most holy, we praise you.

Glory be to you, most Holy God – Father, Son and Holy Spirit. Bless the worship we offer you this day; join our prayers and our songs to those of Christ our Lord, in whose name we pray. **Amen.**

Easter

Creator God we praise you, for you took us from the dust of the earth and gave us the breath of life.

Creator God, we praise you.

Jesus our brother we worship you, for you laid your life down that death may no longer have the last say over our mortal bodies.

Jesus our brother, we worship you.

Spirit most holy we praise you, for you breathe the living future of God into dead bodies and communities and churches.

Spirit most holy, we praise you.

Easter

O Christ the Stranger, Christ the wounded and the weak,

We greet you!

Christ the Teacher, Christ the Wisdom of God,

We praise you!

Christ the Living One, risen to blaze a trail for us into that land flowing with milk and honey,

We worship you!

Easter

Lord of life, good Shepherd of the sheep, we praise you for your care of us. Where would we be without the shelter of your love? What good purpose could our lives possibly have served apart from your example? This morning we come with joy to listen to your words and treasure them in our hearts. Fill us with a living hope that the day of your justice will indeed arrive. We long for that day when the hungry will no longer be hungry, and the thirsty will no longer be parched. In your mercy, guide us all to the water of life and wipe away our tears forever.

Amen.

Easter

We praise you God most high with sun moon and stars.
With sun and sky, with rain and hail, snow and frost and stormy gale, we praise you.
We praise you with mountain and hill, with trees and their fruits, with animals that creep and slither, with birds on the wing.
We praise you with all the company of God's people, women and men, young and old.
We praise you because you are love, and command us to love one another.
We praise you because, through Jesus' resurrection from the dead, you have made all things new.
We praise you because you make clean everything that is unclean.
We praise you that one day we shall live with you in a new heaven and a new earth, when death and pain shall be no more and every tear shall be wiped away.
Most High God we praise you – Father, Son and Holy Spirit.
All glory and honour is yours for ever and ever.

As we gather now to worship, we humbly ask that you would send your Spirit upon us, that through a careful listening to your word we might be encouraged to become your people more and more and to follow more nearly in the footsteps of our saviour Jesus. This we ask in Jesus name, and for his sake. **Amen.**

Pentecost or Ordinary Time

Come Holy Spirit, wild willy-wind of God;
when we studiously ignore your claims on our lives,
please don't take no for an answer!
Come Holy Spirit, come change our hearts.

Come Holy Spirit, friend of Jesus and living water;
when our lives become dry and barren and deadly,
surprise us with your falling showers of joy.
Come Holy Spirit, come change our hearts.

Come Holy Spirit, friend of nomads, apostles and saints;
when our lives have become habitual to the point of absurdity,
drag us into pilgrimage with you.
Take us with you into the strange and dangerous places of God.
Come Holy Spirit, come change our hearts.

Pentecost

Come Creator Spirit, earth-maker and story-teller,
breathe new life into our tired imaginations;
give us eyes to see your artistry and ears to hear your truth.
Come, Holy Spirit, come change our hearts.

Come Spirit of Jesus, friend and comforter,
breathe new life into our fatigued compassion;
enlarge our love for all who are suffering, poor, or lost.
Come, Holy Spirit, come change our hearts.

Come Spirit of the church, muse of prophets and holy fire,
breathe new life into our weary discipleship;
make us poor again, that we may remember we are rich;
give us your cross again, that we may remember your gift of life.
Come Holy Spirit, come change our hearts.

Great God of promise – Father, Son and Holy Spirit – accept the praise we offer in this place. By your never-failing love, grant us the faith of Abraham and Sarah, faith enough to follow wherever you would lead us, even unto the 'better country' you have promised. Glory be to you, great God, glory be. **Amen.**

Pentecost or Ordinary Time

Come Holy Spirit, breath of God and author of life:
Come Holy Spirit, make us alive!

Come Holy Spirit, re-designer of Christ's broken body:
Come Holy Spirit, make us alive!

Come Holy Spirit, artist and architect of all peace and joy:
Come Holy Spirit, make us alive!

Pentecost

Holy Spirit,
you are the Lord, the giver of life;
with the Father and the Son we worship and glorify you:
come to us now, Spirit of God.

Holy Spirit,
you were there at the creation before time began;
your presence fills the whole universe:
come to us now, Spirit of life.

Holy Spirit,
you have spoken through the prophets of old;
by their witness the Word of God has never been silent:
come to us now, Spirit of wisdom.

Holy Spirit,
you surrounded the waiting Church with the wind of Pentecost;
you gave life and breath to announce Christ's gospel:
come to us now, Spirit of power.

Holy Spirit,
you came upon the first Christians as a holy fire;
you set their hearts ablaze with devotion to the risen Lord:
Come to us now, loving Spirit.

Holy Spirit,
you pour out your rich and varied gifts;
you call us to bring forth your fruit in our lives:
Come to us now, gracious Spirit.

Holy Spirit,
you are the Spirit of truth, the Counsellor;
you lead us to the truth that sets us free:
Come to us now, Spirit of God,
and renew Christ's holy Church.

Trinity

Father of Love,
who made the world in your likeness to be a community of hospitality and peace:
With our lips we praise you!

Christ risen and ascended,
Christ who bears our sin and failure so that injustice and despair may be ended for ever:
With our bodies we worship you!

Spirit most Holy,
animating the church that the whole creation might also be made alive in your love:
With all our hearts we welcome you!

Trinity

Mother of creation, who stirred the waters of chaos and, by your primal Word,
called the universe into being,
Come now to make this world new!

Christ our brother, who suffered our most hideous evils,
and yet loved us with a love that is stronger than death,
Come now to fill us with rejoicing!

Spirit of life, who midwives your church through the pain of labour
into the wide open spaces of resurrection joy.
Come now to enliven your people!

God most holy, one in three and three in one,
you are our beginning, our middle, and our end.
In you is the life that animates the stars
and fills the hungry bellies of your broken people.
We worship and adore you for ever and ever. **Amen.**

Ordinary Time

What a strange God you are, Yahweh of Israel! Your people looked to you for miracles and wonders, sure signs that you were a strong and mighty king who would always be willing to intervene on their behalf. But all you gave was the sign of the cross: a powerless man hanging naked on a cross.

What a strange God you are, Yahweh of Israel! The Romans and the Greeks looked to you for oracles of wisdom, fine words able to penetrate to the heart of things, magnificent equations by which to measure the breadth and depths of the mysteries of our existence. But all you gave them was the sign of the cross: a fool rendered mute by the pain of his crucifixion.

Yet, for all its absurdities, the sign of the cross has become, for us, the very source of our salvation. For it was there that we heard your wisest and most powerful word. “In the cross,” you told us, “I have acted decisively for everyone who is neither strong nor wise, as the world would understand these things. In the cross I chose the foolish to shame those who think they are wise; in the cross I chose the weak, the poor, and the marginalised to shame those who considered themselves strong. In the cross I taught the world a lesson it is still struggling to learn: that the blessed ones are those who know only one thing: that I love them, that I am merciful.”

God our Father, we praise you for the cross of Christ. For when your son was swept from your arms by a deluge of rotten religion and corrupt politics, we found what we were looking for: a God who could forgive us.

We praise you, strange God – Father, Son and Holy Spirit – and adore you for ever. **Amen.**

Ordinary Time

Voice 1: Hail to the Maker, the Ancient One,
Mother and Father of all that was, and is, and will be!
Today we join with birds and trees and animals,
with rocks and rivers and mountains and the whole creation
to offer you our worship and honour.
Come to us, God of Life! We invoke you!
Come to fill us with your creative power,
with the pulsing lifeblood of ages.
Make us alive with celebration and with rejoicing!

Voice 2: Hail to the Christ, the Compassionate One,
who was alive and was dead and now lives in the heart of all things!
In the midnight of sin, you heard the cries of your people.

For us and for our healing,
you embraced that darkness with its loneliness and despair;
you surrendered to the crack which rends the cosmos.
Come to us, Suffering One! We invoke you!
Renew our yearning for emptiness and for silence.

Voice 3: Hail to the Spirit Holy, messenger of God's Wisdom,
primal fire of creation and breath of life!
From the time of dreaming you made your home with holy souls,
making them friends of God and prophets.
You invite us to join with you in the circle dance of trinity,
to die and be reborn in the whirling wheel of God.
Come to us, Spirit of Life! We invoke you!
Renew your people in the passion of the ancients:
make of us mystics and poets and prophets,
that the earth may be rekindled in love.

Blessed be God—Father, Son and Holy Spirit—
As in the beginning, so now, and for ever. Amen.

Ordinary Time

God of exiles: when your word was read aloud by Ezra the priest,
your people wept with both sorrow and joy:
Come, God of exiles,
renew us by your word and your Spirit!

Lord Jesus Christ: in you the word of your Father became flesh and dwelt among us.
By your preaching and your love, you set us free and healed all our wounds.
Come, Lord Jesus,
renew us by your word and your Spirit!

Breath of heaven: from diverse places, times, gifts and ministries,
you gather your people into one body by which you make known the word of life.
Come, breath of heaven,
renew us by your word and your Spirit!

Loving God—Father, Son and Holy Spirit—come now to do with us what you did with your people of old. By your mercy, make us your hands and feet and voice for a world in peril. In Christ's name we pray. **Amen.**

Ordinary Time

Blessed are you, God of the prophets. You knew Jeremiah even before he was born and chose him to be your voice in a difficult time. He built a community of truth where there was only lies, and renewed the spirit of hope where there was only evil and despair.

Come, blessed Father,
fill your people with the faith of the prophets.

Blessed are you, Jesus our brother. You stood up to become your Father's voice for a despairing people. You gave courage and faith to the poor and forgotten. You called the smug and the powerful to compassion and truthfulness.

Come, blessed Jesus,
fill your people with power to hope.

Blessed are you, Spirit of love. You come in every time and place to empower your people for prophecy. Fill us with yourself, that our faith, hope and love may be renewed – both in prayer and in action.

Come, blessed Spirit,
fill your people with courage to love.

Blessed are you most loving God – Father, Son and Holy Spirit – now and for ever. ***Amen.***

Ordinary Time

We praise you, God of mercy.
With compassion you rescue the widow and the orphan from their hunger and despair.

God of mercy, come now to pour out your kindness.

We praise you, Jesus, friend of mourners.
Your heart goes out to all who have been separated from their loved ones.
You bring mercy and healing to everyone who is broken.

Jesus, friend of mourners, come now to offer your comfort.

We praise you, Spirit of revelation.
In love you let even us into the secret of the ages:
that God was in Christ, calling the world into God's arms of welcome.
Spirit of revelation, come now to tell the good news!

Ordinary Time

God of Elijah, quiet whisperer of peace and of encouragement:
come now, still our fearful hearts and minds that we may be ready to eat your words of comfort and drink your cup of salvation.

Jesus our friend, liberator of demoniacs and restorer of health:
come now, still our anxious hearts and minds that we may be ready to receive your words of healing and of hope.

Spirit of holiness, defender of the just and revealer of all light and truth:
come now, still the voices of accusation in us that we may be ready to own your gracious gift of lovingkindness.

God most holy – Father, Son and Holy Spirit –
it is you we love, you we praise, you we adore for ever and ever. **Amen.**

Ordinary Time or Pentecost

Come Holy Spirit, still, silent breath of God,
meet our tense and anxious worrying
with the quiet whispering of your peace.
Come, Holy Spirit, come breath of God.

Come Holy Spirit, water of life,
touch our burning angers, our frustrations and heartaches,
with the soothing streams of your affection.
Come, Holy Spirit, come water of life.

Come Holy Spirit, dove of heaven and wings of God,
raise these eyes, so downcast and sullen,
raise them to the horizon of your flight,
to the east and to the light,
where your beauty creeps silently into the world.
Come Holy Spirit, come dove of God.

Great God of love – Father, Son and Holy Spirit – as we gather to worship you together this morning, we ask that you would bless us with your presence and a knowledge of your will, that we might follow Christ more nearly and love him more dearly, day by day. **Amen.**

Refugee Sunday

God of Israel, you rescued your people from slavery in Egypt and made them a refuge for everyone whose homes have been destroyed.

Come Lord, be our strength and refuge.

Jesus, son of humanity, you came to announce God's good news for the poor, to tell them that their time of tears is coming to an end.

Come Lord, be our light and salvation.

Spirit of justice, you make us citizens of heaven and strangers to the world. Come Lord, fill us with yearning for your reign of justice and peace.

Come Lord, be our strength and refuge.

Reign of Christ

Faithful God, who set David on the throne of Israel and made of him a model and a paradigm of the good and righteous ruler: come now to all who are poor and struggling with life to show us your reign of mercy and care.

Come now, faithful God.

Faithful Witness, who stood before Pilate and spoke of a kingdom that comes from somewhere else, a kingdom that values truth, not lies, and love, not slavery: come now to all who are drowning in lies and hatred, come now to set them free.

Come now, faithful witness.

Faithful Spirit, who dances before the throne in heaven and empowers all the faithful to bear witness to your coming rule: come now to all who feel weak and worthless and give them the gentle power of priests and kings, that by their words and their actions Christ's reign of peace may arrive in our world.

Come now, faithful Spirit.

Reign of Christ

Father most merciful, great shepherd of your people Israel,
come like a mother with her child at the breast:

**Come, tender God,
gather us into your kingdom of loving kindness.**

Jesus our brother, firstborn of all creation and suffering messiah,
come like a reaper, longing for that harvest of justice:

**Come, merciful Reaper,
gather us into your kingdom of peace.**

Spirit most holy, heart of the prophets and revealer of truth,
come like a wind, like a dove bearing good news,

Come, breath of God,
gather us into your kingdom of light.

God most high – Father, Son and Holy Spirit – it is you we praise this day: for making this world so mysterious and fruitful, for revealing yourself in song and in prophecy, for coming amongst us as a prince and true shepherd of your people Israel. Bless the worship be offer this day and make it true. **Amen.**

LAMENT/CONFESSION/ABSOLUTION

Advent

Let us open our hearts and prepare for his coming, confessing our sins in penitence and faith.

Because we are busy to prepare for the holidays,
but lazy to prepare for your coming,
Lord, have mercy: **Lord, have mercy.**

Because we are awake with our buying
but asleep with our prayer,
Christ, have mercy: **Christ, have mercy.**

Because we have forgotten the Advent disciplines,
because they are crowded out by end of year functions
and Christmas celebrations that arrive too early,
Lord, have mercy: **Lord, have mercy.**

Christmas

Loving Lord, today the light of Christ has dawned upon us. Forgive us, then, when we allow the despair and darkness of our world to dim that light, to steal away our Christmas faith, hope and joy.

(sung:) **Kyrie eleison . . .**

Lord Christ, today you were born to the manger and to poverty. Forgive us, then, when we treat Christmas as a time to enrich ourselves, giving only to those who may give in return.

(sung:) **Christe eleison . . .**

Gentle Spirit, this is the day when the Shepherds put their work aside in order to adore the Christ at the place of his birth. Forgive us, then, when our Christmas activities are so frenetic that there is little time for worship or wonder.

(sung:) **Kyrie eleison . . .**

Listen to the word of the Angel of God:
'Do not be afraid, for see, I bring you good news of great joy for all the people: to you is born this day, in the city of David, a Saviour who is Christ the Lord.'

Luke 2:10, 11

Christ therefore has this word of grace for anyone who would turn to him with a soul broken or wounded by sin: 'Your sins are forgiven.'

Thanks be to God!

Christmas

Because Christ has come amongst us,
bone of our bone, and flesh of our flesh:

(sung): **Kyrie eleison . . .**

Because he is our peace, breaking down the barriers that divide us from you and each other:

(sung): **Christ eleision . . .**

Because he has made us children of God,
and heirs of all that you promised us through your holy prophets:

(sung): **Kyrie eleison . . .**

Listen to the word of the Angel of God:
Do not be afraid, for see, I bring you good news of great joy for all the people: to you is born this day, in the city of David, a Saviour who is Christ the Lord.

Luke 2:10, 11

Christ therefore has this word of grace for anyone who would turn to him with a soul broken or wounded by sin:

'Your sins are forgiven.' **Thanks be to God!**

Epiphany

Lord, because our worship of Christ is like that of Herod sometimes; naming him 'Lord' with our lips, but failing to honour him in our lives,

Lord have mercy: **Lord have mercy.**

Jesus, because we offer such tardy gifts to you, gifts that do not cost us anything, gifts that we value little ourselves,

Christ, have mercy: **Christ, have mercy.**

Lord, because we do not believe in your mystery sometimes, the mystery of the Word made flesh, the Light that is shining to save the whole world from its darkness,

Lord, have mercy: **Lord, have mercy.**

Listen to the word of Christ:
I am the light of the world. Whoever follows me will never walk in darkness, but shall have the light of life.

John 8:12

Christ therefore has this word of grace for everyone who wants to turn from their darkness and follow the light of Christ: 'Your sins are forgiven.' **Thanks be to God!**

Epiphany

When we hear your call to follow Christ crucified, but respond with hesitation,

Lord, have mercy: **Lord, have mercy.**

When we hear your call to love all people, but respond with excuses and clever escape clauses,

Christ, have mercy: **Christ, have mercy.**

When we hear your call to prayer, but respond by filling every available space with noise and frenetic activity,

Lord, have mercy: **Lord, have mercy.**

Hear the word of the Psalmist:
As for me, I am poor and needy, but the Lord takes thought for me. The Lord is my help and deliverer.

Psalm 40:17

Hear, then, Christ's word of grace for all who come to him with a broken and contrite spirit:

'Your sins are forgiven!' **Thanks be to God.**

Baptism of Jesus

Because we doubt your creative power in our lives, because we entertain the fantasy that we can do it all on our own,

Lord have mercy: **Lord, have mercy.**

Because we have sanitised the life of Christ, turning it into a moral fable which is no longer able to change the way we live in the present,
Christ have mercy: **Christ, have mercy.**

Because we resist the power of the Spirit in our lives, the Spirit who cries out "Abba, Father" and makes us your beloved children,
Lord have mercy: **Lord, have mercy.**

Listen to the word of the Prophet:
Do not be afraid, I have called you by name. You are mine. When you pass through the waters, I shall be with you. When you pass through the flames, you shall not be harmed.

Isaiah 43:1-2

Christ has this word of grace, then, for all who come to him with a broken and contrite spirit: 'Your sins are forgiven'. **Thanks be to God!**

Lent

In a moment of quiet, let us confess to God the truth about the world and ourselves. Let us ask God for help, that we may see ourselves clearly . . .

Because we are so easily deceived by the appearance of things,
Lord, have mercy: **Lord, have mercy.**

Because we so often fail to grab hold of the life that you offer us,
Christ, have mercy: **Christ, have mercy.**

Because we would rather believe in fate that in your power to save,
Lord, have mercy: **Lord, have mercy.**

Listen to the word of the Psalmist:

If you, O Lord, should keep a record of wrongs, who could stand? But there is forgiveness with you, that you might be honoured. My soul waits for the Lord, and in his word I hope.

Psalm 130:3-5

Christ has this word of grace, then, for everyone who dares to hope in the power of his steadfast love and welcome:
'Your sins are forgiven'. **Thanks be to God!**

Lent

God our father, you long to save us from our bondage to *things*. Yet we love our *things*, even more than we love you.

Lord, have mercy: **Lord, have mercy.**

Saviour Jesus, you came to quench our thirst with the truth of your love. Yet we persist in deceiving ourselves. We persist in hankering after the *things* that cannot satisfy.

Christ, have mercy: **Christ, have mercy.**

Holy Spirit, you are promised to us as food for the journey and grace for the road. Yet, very often, we would prefer not even to travel with you. We would prefer to stay at home and risk nothing.

Lord, have mercy: **Lord, have mercy.**

Listen to the word of the Apostle:
God proves his love for us in this. It was while we were still sinners that Christ died for us.

Romans 5:8

Christ has this word of grace, then, for anyone who, willing to admit their deep need, is willing to turn to him for mercy and help:

'Your sins are forgiven'. **Thanks be to God!**

Lent

Father God,
you sent Jesus not to condemn, but to save and heal us.
Forgive us, then, when we condemn both ourselves and each other.
Lord, have mercy: **Lord, have mercy.**

Lord Jesus Christ,
you came amongst us as one who longs for our release
and liberation into the freedom of God's children.
Forgive us, then, when we would rather stay bound,
tied up in the pressure to accumulate and perform.
Christ, have mercy: **Christ, have mercy.**

Spirit most Holy,
you came to befriend and encourage us on the road to freedom.
Forgive us, then, we turn aside from your encouragement,
and crush all your dreams for us into very small boxes.
Lord, have mercy: **Lord, have mercy.**

Listen to the word of Jesus Christ:
God loved the world so much, that he sent his only Son, so that everyone who trusts in him may not perish, but live in eternal life.

John 3:16

Christ has this word of grace, then, for everyone who comes to him with a desire to change, to put off the old ways and put on the new:

'Your sins are forgiven.' **Thanks be to God!**

Lent

Lord of Love,
Because, in the face of flood and fire, we so often put aside your promise of life and, instead, give in to the fear that we shall lose everything that is really important.

Lord, have mercy: **Lord, have mercy.**

Because, in our longing for importance and security, we so often forget the power of your Spirit to make us son and daughters of the most high God:

Christ, have mercy: **Christ, have mercy.**

Because, in our thirst for meaningful lives, we so often place our trust not in the cleansing, healing, waters of Christ, but in the powers and principalities that rule our world:

Lord, have mercy: **Lord, have mercy.**

Listen to the word of the Psalmist:
Good and upright is the LORD; therefore he instructs sinners in the way. He leads the humble in what is right, and teaches the humble God's way.

Psalm 25:8-9

Christ has this word of grace, then, for everyone who would turn from their sin and seek God's mercy:

'Your sins are forgiven.' **Thanks be to God!**

Easter

In a moment of quiet, let us confess to God all that holds us back from the freefall of faith in his Risen Jesus.

A moment of quiet is observed.

Lord of the living and the dead:

Because we treat the resurrection as a nice story which yet has no real power to interrupt and convert our lives,

Lord have mercy: **Lord, have mercy.**

Because we would rather be miserable than embrace the joy of your resurrection life,

Christ have mercy: **Christ, have mercy.**

Because we would prefer a tamer god, a more domesticated god, a god nicely contained in the tomb of our small-mindedness,

Lord have mercy: **Lord, have mercy.**

Listen to the word of the Apostle:
Repent and be baptised, every one of you, in the name of Jesus Christ, so that your sins may be forgiven; and you will receive the gift of the Holy Spirit. This is a promise for you, and for everyone; for God calls everyone to his side.

Acts 2:38, 39

Christ has this word of grace, then, for everyone who has doubted God's power, for everyone who now would turn to Christ for help and strength to transform their lives:

'Your sins are forgiven.' **Thanks be to God!**

Easter

Because we are afraid to die, and so be raised with Christ:

Lord, have mercy: **Lord, have mercy.**

Because we are afraid to lose everything, and so gain everything in Christ:

Christ, have mercy: **Christ, have mercy.**

Because we fear death by water, because we are afraid to be reborn to Christ's new world:

Lord have mercy: **Lord, have mercy.**

Listen to the word of the Apostle:
They put Jesus to death by hanging him on a tree; but God raised him on the third day and allowed him to appear, not to all the people but to us who were chosen by God as witnesses, and who ate and drank with him after he rose from the dead . . . All the prophets testify about him that everyone who believes in him receives forgiveness of sins through his name.

Acts 10:39-43

Listen, then, to the word of Christ to everyone who, recognizing that all is not well with their lives, would turn to him for mercy and help:

'Your sins are forgiven.' **Thanks be to God!**

Easter

Gracious Father, because we are sometimes afraid of your love, because we would sometimes rather punish ourselves than accept that we are loved;

Lord, have mercy: **Lord, have mercy.**

Christ our brother, because we are so often too busy to sit with you, and feel your tender embrace; because we drive ourselves hard in order to feel worthy enough;

Christ, have mercy: **Christ, have mercy.**

Spirit most holy, because we are sometimes afraid even of life, because we are so often seduced into believing that only a practised numbness may deliver us from the suffering we endure;

Lord, have mercy: **Lord, have mercy.**

Listen to the word of the apostle:
'Christ suffered for sin, the righteous one for the unrighteous many, in order to bring you to God. He was put to death in the body, but made alive in the Spirit . . .'

1 Pet 3:18

Therefore Christ has this word of grace for everyone who, knowing that they are dead in their sins, would look to him for life where there is none:

'Your sins are forgiven'. **Thanks be to God!**

Pentecost

Loving Lord, hear the truth of who we are.

You call us to be people of integrity, where words and actions agree with each other. But our tongues often claim too much, so that our deeds are left to languish in the shadows of our failure.

Lord have mercy: **Lord, have mercy.**

In Jesus you showed us how to be born again, to live as though nothing else mattered except the life of your Spirit. But so often we forget to listen for the quiet whisper of your call within us. So often we allow ourselves to be carried along by other voices, voices of greed and envy and the service of self.

Christ have mercy: **Christ, have mercy.**

You call us to be your children, to live according to the freedom of your Spirit within us. Yet our courage sometimes fails us. It is so much easier to follow the crowd, to bind ourselves to the common-sense and the common-place.

Lord, have mercy: **Lord, have mercy.**

Listen to the words of Jesus, our Lord:
'God so loved the world that he gave his only Son, so that everyone who believes in him may not perish, but have eternal life. For God did not send the Son into the world to condemn the world, but in order that the world might be saved through him.'

John 3:16, 17

Here, then, Christ's word of grace toward everyone who turns away from their sin and towards Christ in faith, hope and love:

'Your sins are forgiven.' **Thanks be to God!**

Trinity

God our mother and father, you made the world to be a community of love. Yet so often we find ourselves lashing out at one another, nation against nation, man against woman, humankind against nature.

Lord, have mercy: **Lord, have mercy.**

Jesus, you commissioned your church to make disciples of all nations, baptising them in the name of God and teaching them to obey everything that you taught us. Yet so often we put this great mission aside in favour of more trivial pursuits.

Christ, have mercy: **Christ, have mercy.**

Holy Spirit, you were sent into the world to make us one with the Father and the Son in the communion of divine love. Yet your church is not as one. Though we share the one Lord, the one faith, and the one baptism, we grieve that we are not yet able to share together at the Lord's table.

Lord, have mercy: **Lord, have mercy.**

Listen to the words of John the Evangelist:

Jesus breathed on the disciples and said to them, 'Receive the Holy Spirit. If you forgive the sins of any, they are forgiven them.'

John 20:22, 23

Christ has this word of grace, therefore, for anyone who stops pretending that all is well with their lives, and who turns to Christ for mercy and help:

'Your sins are forgiven.' **Thanks be to God!**

Reconciliation Week

Because, deep in our hearts, we remain mistrustful of the one who is different to ourselves, who comes from another ethnicity and another understanding,

Lord, have mercy. **Lord, have mercy.**

Because we are more inclined to affirm the notion of reconciliation because it is politically correct, than to get involved in making reconciliation happen,

Christ, have mercy. **Christ, have mercy.**

Because we have not yet learned the power of forgiveness,
either for ourselves or for our nation,

Lord, have mercy. **Lord, have mercy.**

Hear the word of the apostle:
Christ is our peace. In his body he has broken down the dividing wall, the hostility between us. He has abolished the law, with its commandments and ordinances, that he might create in himself one new humanity, thus making peace, reconciling all of us to God in one body through the cross.

Ephesians 2:14-16

Christ has this word of grace for all who would seek to be reconciled to neighbour and to God:

'Your sins are forgiven.' **Thanks be to God.**

Refugee Sunday

In a moment of quiet, let us to confess to God who we really are in all our fear, our brokenness, our sin, knowing that God loves and welcomes everyone who is lost and cannot find a home . . .

Lord, you welcome the stranger and the alien without condition.
But we, so often, welcome only those whom we know and love.
(sung): *Kyrie eleison.*

Jesus, you love and accept all who were weak and vulnerable.
But so often we love only what is strong, confident and 'successful'.
(sung): *Christe eleison.*

Lord, you welcome us without condition; you forgive our sins and make a home for us in your heart. Forgive us when we forget your mercy and wander, again, into the trackless wastes of our world.
(sung): *Kyrie eleison.*

Listen to the experience of the Psalmist:
God will hide me in his shelter in the day of trouble; he will conceal me under the cover of his tent; he will set me high on a rock, so that my enemies cannot reach me.

Psalm 27:5

Listen, then, for Christ's word of grace to everyone who turns to God for mercy and help in the day of trouble:
'Your sins are forgiven.' **Thanks be to God.**

Ordinary Time

Because we do whatever takes our fancy rather than listening, expectantly, for your voice of invitation and promise,
Lord, have mercy: **Lord, have mercy.**

Because we do whatever is easy and comfortable rather than submitting to your uncomfortable and costly grace,
Christ, have mercy: **Christ, have mercy.**

Because, when your come looking for us, it is so often the case than we would rather not be found,
Lord, have mercy: **Lord, have mercy.**

Listen to the word of the apostle:
The saying is sure and worthy of full acceptance, that Jesus Christ came into the world to save sinners—of whom I am the foremost. But that is why I received mercy, so that in me Jesus might display the utmost patience, making me an example for all who would come to believe in him.

1 Tim 1:15, 16

Therefore, Christ has this word of grace for all who cease to pretend that they don't need God, for all who turn to God for grace and mercy in their time of need:

'Your sins are forgiven.' **Thanks be to God!**

Ordinary Time

God of blessing,
we read in holy Scripture that you are sovereign over all creation.
Yet, when we look at the world around us, oftentimes we doubt.
Lord, have mercy: **Lord have mercy.**

We read in holy Scripture that we are witnesses of the resurrection.
Yet so often we keep our mouths firmly shut.
Christ, have mercy: **Christ have mercy.**

We read in Holy Scripture that you are sending your Spirit to give us power and hope for our mission. Yet, sometimes we despair.
Lord, have mercy: **Lord have mercy.**

Listen to the word of the apostle:
'God has put all things under Christ's feet and has made him the head over all things for the church, which is his body, the fullness of him who fills all in all.'

Ephesians 1:22, 23

Hear then Christ's word of grace for all who struggle to see that it is so:

'Your sins are forgiven'. **Thanks be to God!**

Ordinary Time

God most holy, sometimes we doubt that you love us.
Life gets difficult and our faith grows weak.
Forgive us.

Jesus our brother, sometimes you invite us into the joy of new life but we miss the invitation because we are too preoccupied with worrying.
Heal us.

Spirit of life, you stand before us offering nothing but life, life in all its fullness.
Forgive us, then, when we refuse your gift out of shame or fear.
Bind up our wounds.

Listen, everyone, to the word of the prophet:
'No longer will my people be called 'deserted' or 'desolate'. Instead you will be called 'God's delight' and 'God's spouse'. For as a young man takes marries a maiden, so the Lord will marry you; as the bridegroom rejoices over his bride, so the Lord will rejoice over you.'

Isaiah 62:4, 5

Hear then Christ's word of grace toward everyone calls out to him when the day of trouble comes:
'Go in peace. Your sins are forgiven': **Thanks be to God!**

Ordinary Time

Lord of love:
Forgive us when we doubt your care for us,
when we can see only what is going wrong rather than what is going right.
Lord, have mercy: **Lord, have mercy.**

Forgive us when we would keep the good news of your love to ourselves,
instead of sharing it liberally with all who are broken or afraid.
Christ, have mercy: **Christ, have mercy.**

Forgive us when we would rather worship death than life,
allowing people to slip away into isolation and despair instead of supporting them
to find life within the bosom of a compassionate community.
Lord, have mercy: **Lord, have mercy.**

Listen to the word of the gospel:
'A great prophet has appeared among us. God has looked with favour on his people.'

Luke 7:16

Hear, then, Christ's word of grace to everyone who is bound up in sin, cut off from the compassion of God because of human cruelty and neglect:
'Your sins are forgiven.' **Thanks be to God!**

Ordinary Time

Because we neglect the widows, the orphans and the refugees,
Lord have mercy: **Lord have mercy.**

Because we fail to bring our fears and anxieties, our heartaches and our failures, before you in prayer,

Christ have mercy: **Christ have mercy.**

Because we forget to rest, to make Sabbath, and to listen for your voice of grace, comfort and peace,

Lord have mercy: **Lord have mercy.**

Listen to the word of the Apostle:
God has rescued us from the power of darkness and transplanted us into the kingdom of his beloved Son, in whom we have redemption, the forgiveness of our sins.

Colossians 1:13

Therefore, Christ has this word of grace for all who come to him with a broken and contrite spirit:

'Your sins are forgiven.' **Thanks be to God!**

Ordinary Time

Lord, you give our lives, our work, our families and friends, and even the air we breathe as a gift of grace. But we live as though we produced all these wonders for ourselves.

Lord, have mercy: **Lord, have mercy.**

Jesus, you taught us to share with the poor, the weak and the wretched, with those who cannot repay. But we busy ourselves with caring for those from whom we may expect a return of praise and gratitude.

Christ, have mercy: **Christ, have mercy.**

Lord, you call us to offer hospitality to the stranger, to the one who is least like ourselves. But we are birds of a feather who like to flock together. We find it difficult to make ourselves vulnerable like that.

Lord, have mercy: **Lord, have mercy.**

Listen to the word of the Apostle:
God has promised 'never will I leave or forsake you.' That is why we can say, with confidence: 'The Lord is my helper; I will not be afraid. What can a mere human being do to me?'

Hebrews 13:5b, 6

Christ has this word of grace, then, for everyone who stops pretending that he or she has it together—for everyone who acknowledges the truth about themselves and turns to Christ for help:

'Your sins are forgiven'. **Thanks be to God!**

Reign of Christ

Lord of love, forgive us. When the leaders we want are not elected, or when the leaders we elect disappoint, we sometimes forget that you yourself are our shepherd, and that it is you, yourself, who will care for us.

Be merciful, Lord.

Lord of love, forgive us. When the world seems dark and cold, when nation takes up sword against nation and the children of God seem powerless to do anything about it, help us to remember your promise: that no power in heaven or on earth will ever be able to separate us from your love.

Be merciful, Lord.

Lord of love, forgive us. When we feel lost in the world, forgotten by governments and friends alike, remind us that we are your beloved children, heirs with Jesus of everything that is yours. In Jesus you have already given us everything that we could ever need to be blessed. Remind us of your promise to Julian of Norwich: that all shall be well, and that all things shall be well.

Be merciful, Lord.

Listen to the song of the Psalmist:
The Lord has chosen Zion for his dwelling place . . . I will bless her with abundant provision, I will satisfy her poor with food and dress her priests with salvation. Her saints shall ever sing for joy!

Psalm 132:13, 16,

Hear, then, Christ's promise of mercy to all who acknowledge Christ's kingship:

'Your sins are forgiven'. **Thanks be to God.**

OCCASIONAL PRAYERS FOR USE IN THE PRAYERS OF THE PEOPLE

Christmas

God of Jesus, on this Eve of our Lord's Nativity we praise you for the extraordinary depth of your love for us. When all the lights had gone out in the world, when the hopes and dreams of your people had come to nothing, you sent your Son to be the light of the world. In his light despair could hold sway no longer. In his light the poor and the dispossessed found firm grounds for hope. In his light our sins were driven away. In his light that forgotten future of peace with justice became possible again.

And so we pray for the church and the world, that all may be bathed in the transfiguring peace of the Christ-child:

God of Emmanuel, Light from Light,
Come set your people free.

Recalling the joy of the Shepherds, how they went amongst their people praising God for all they had seen and heard, we pray for the church of Jesus Christ: that we may take the heart of Christ to *our* hearts, bearing witness in all that we say and do to the vision of Christ for our world. Lord, in your mercy, grant us courage in these dark and difficult times to choose the way of Jesus. Save us from the constant temptation to do what is easy or expedient, rather than what is right. Give your church the Spirit of Christ, that we may cheerfully follow him through trial and cross to resurrection and glory, even unto the banqueting room of heaven.

God of Emmanuel, Light from Light,
Come set your people free.

Recalling that Christ was born into a world dominated by the power and paranoia of one man, the Emperor of Rome, we pray for the leaders of our world, an especially for the Secretary-General of the United Nations, Ban Ki-moon. By your apostles and prophets, teach our political leaders the story of a God who does not cling to power, but gives it away; show them that if they treat their enemies like friends, then their enemies may *become* their friends; teach him the infinite value of giving and of sharing.

God of Emmanuel, Light from Light,
Come set your people free.

Recalling that Christ was born not in a palace, but in a barn, we pray today for all who live in poverty . . . By the faithfulness of Christian preachers and prophets, tell them the story of Christ's love for all who are poor, marginalised or forgotten. By the action of deacons, and other agents of practical compassion, show them that while others may have forgotten them, *you* have not forgotten them.

God of Emmanuel, Light from Light,
Come set your people free.

Recalling the message of the Angel, that Christ was born both Lord and Messiah, we pray for our kin in messianic faith, the Jews. With them we pray earnestly for the Day of the Lord to arrive, the day when Christ shall come to shake the greedy from their thrones and lift up all who have suffered long in faith, in hope and in charity. In the meantime, we pray for the peace of Jerusalem and for the healing of all those who continue to suffer the Shoah, even now, these many years later.

God of Emmanuel, Light from Light,
Come set your people free.

Finally, Lord, recalling that Christ came amongst us as bone of our bone and flesh of our flesh, we pray for those we know and love who could use a touch from you right now. We pray for all who are sick, whether in body of mind. We pray for all whose spirits have been all but crushed by the oppressive consumerism of this season. We pray for all who have lost their homes in bushfires. Make yourself known to them, Lord. In their darkness, shine the light of your love . . .

God of Emmanuel, Light from Light,
Come set your people free.

God Most High,
your Son Jesus embraced the frailty of our flesh
that we may receive power to become your children.
He chose to dwell amongst us that we might come to dwell with you,
at the very beating of your heart.
Grant us, this Christmas Eve, lives of thanksgiving
that we may evermore praise you for the gift of your Son,
and live our lives after his image and likeness;
he who lives and reigns with you in the unity of the Holy Spirit,
one God for ever and ever. **Amen.**

All Saints or All Souls

God of the ages,
we praise you for all your servants who have done justice,
loved mercy, and walked humbly with their God.
For apostles and martyrs and saints of every time and place,
who in life and in death have witnessed to your love and truth,
God of mercy, we praise you.

For all those Christian disciples who have faithfully served you,
witnessed bravely in the face of persecution, and died in faith,
who, in our memories, still shine as lights in the world,
God of mercy, we praise you.

For those no longer remembered,
who earnestly sought you in dark and harrowing times,
who held fast their faith in trial,
and served others without thought of the cost,
God of mercy, we praise you.

For those we have known and loved,
who by their faithful obedience and steadfast hope,
have shown us the heart and mind of Jesus,
God of mercy, we praise you.

And now we pray for those families of our own community
who have lost loved ones in recent times.
In their mourning, God of love, bring comfort and peace.
Let the memory of these saints who have gone on before
spur us also towards love and good deeds,
and all the more as the day of our liberation draws closer.
God of mercy, we praise you.

And there are others, Lord, others who are gone from our sight,
who yet, we believe, dwell with joy within the light of your love.
So now we observe a time of quiet remembering, lighting candles as if to brighten the world with the recollection of their faithfulness.

> Any who wish may come forward to light a taper in memory of a loved one. Place your taper in the sand, beginning at the centre of the bowls, and then working out to the edges.

Lord God almighty,
You surround us with a great cloud of witnesses.
Only sight prevents us from seeing them,
while daily we enjoy the freedoms, insights, and fruits of compassion
which they, in their following of Christ,
achieved for all ages.
God of mercy, we praise you.

God of all people,
not only the achievement of the great,
but also the kindness of the humble
has touched and influenced our lives for good.
We praise you for all the ordinary saints who helped your kingdom take root and grow amongst us.
We praise you for mothers and grandmothers,
fathers and grandfathers,
common heroes and unsung servants of the kingdom
who have shown us the face of Christ.

God of mercy, we praise you.

They, who once sat at your table on earth,
now sit with you at the banqueting-table of heaven.
May we, like them, put the will of Jesus before our own;
may we follow them in following Christ,
in this life and in the life to come.

All glory, praise and honour are yours, O God,
Father, Son, and Holy Spirit,
as in the beginning, so now and forever. **Amen.**

PREFACES FOR THE GREAT PRAYER OF THANKSGIVING

Advent

. . . We bless you, O God, for you are the creator. You formed us in your image and breathed the spirit of life into us. You delivered our forebears from captivity, made covenant with us, and spoke to us through the prophets who looked for that day when

the mountain of the Lord will be established
and all nations will come streaming to its riches.
There the Lord will teach us his ways
so that we may all walk in his paths.
Then we shall beat our swords into plowshares
and our spears into pruning hooks.
Nation will no longer take up sword against nation
nor will they train for war anymore.

Therefore, with the angels and saints . . .

Holy, holy, holy Lord . .

Blessed are you, O God our joy. For as Jesus came to Jerusalem in days of old, so shall he come again. Not, this time, to be tortured and crucified, but to take up the mantle of his father David in the promised kingdom of light. The night is nearly over, the day is nearly here. Therefore we pray 'Come Lord Jesus Christ' and prepare ourselves anew to receive his gift of life . . .

Advent

. . . We bless you, O God, for you are the creator. You formed us in your image and breathed the spirit of life into us. You delivered our forebears from captivity, made covenant with us, and spoke to us through the prophets who looked for that day

when justice shall roll down like waters
and righteousness like an ever-flowing stream,
when nation shall no longer take up sword against nation
nor learn for war anymore.

Therefore, with angels and saints . . .

Holy, holy, holy Lord . . .

Jesus came singing a song of justice which scatters the proud, pulling down the mighty from their towers of arrogance, and exalting the poor and the humble in their stead. Through Jesus you came to fill the hungry with good things and to send the rich away empty. By his baptism of suffering, death and resurrection, you gave hope to all who walk in darkness. By his coming you gave us the eternal sign of Emmanuel: a God who is with us . . .

Christmas

. . . Blessed are you, O God, and worthy of our greatest praise. For the people who walked in darkness have seen a great light. We rejoice tonight as those who, after a long and difficult drought, are surprised with rain and the reaping of a bumper harvest. Tonight, the yoke of your people's burden and the rod of their oppressor is broken forever. For tonight a child has been born for us, whose name is Wonderful, Counsellor, Mighty God and Prince of Peace. To his kingdom of peace there shall be no end. The throne of his father David is established for ever, a sure and certain hope for the ages.

Therefore with angels and saints . . .

Holy, holy, holy Lord . . .

Blessed are you, O God, and blessed is the One you sent to deliver us. By his birth in a stable, by his life, death, and resurrection he has cast down the mighty from their thrones and lifted up all who are poor and forgotten . . .

Transfiguration

. . . It is our greatest joy to praise you, God our creator. You made light from darkness, setting the sun to rule the day and the moon to illumine the night. The light of your glory casts our sin into relief, but the radiance of your love is able to dispel every shadow.
Therefore, with the angels and saints . . .

Holy, holy, holy Lord . . .

Blessed is Jesus Christ, your Son and our Lord. On the mount his face was transfigured with divine light, a promise of resurrection beyond the dark night of his suffering. For us, and for our salvation, he learned the way of the cross, becoming like us in our depravity that we might become like him in his divine glory.

Transfiguration

. . . It is indeed right to give you our thanks and praise, O God, for you made us in your likeness and gave us a place of honour in this wonderful world. You longed to enjoy a loving relationship with us, face-to-face and soul-to-soul, but we spurned both your call and your care and journeyed off into a far country to commune only with our ourselves. Our instincts for love were corrupted, devolving into a desire to possess and control everything and everyone about us.

We praise you that you did not leave us to our darkness but sent your prophets to remind us of your love and of the blessings that come from seeking your face. When the time was fulfilled you sent us your son, the face of your love. Yet we failed to recognise his glory. Mistaking him for a criminal and a charlatan and strung him up on a cross. We praise you, Lord, that even death could not kill your love for us. We praise you that Jesus rose as your cosmic protest against all that we do to each other in the name of our greed. We praise you that his promise remains the power of liberation for everyone who calls out to him for mercy and help.

Therefore with angels and saints . . .

Ash Wednesday

. . . It is truly right to praise you, O God, for you made us from the dust of the earth, breathed the breath of life into us, and set us amidst the beauty of this world to love and serve your ways. We bless you God because when we rejected your love and ignored your wisdom, you did not reject us. You loved us still and called us to turn again to you in faith and obedience.

Therefore, with angels and saints . . .

Holy, holy, holy Lord . . .

Blessed are you, O God of glory, and blessed is your son Jesus Christ our Lord. Out of your great love for the world you sent Jesus amongst us to show us how to live and to set us free from the tyranny of evil. By his life, his death and his resurrection, he released us from our bondage to decay and set us free to live in the freedom of God's children . . .

Lent

. . . It is indeed right to give you our thanks and praise, O God, for you made covenant with Abram and Sarai when they were old and life seemed spent. 'This is my promise' you said. 'I will make from your loins a multitude of nations'. Abraham believed you, despite his great age, and so you called him your righteous one. In this way, against both reason and nature, you gave birth to the way and the family of faith. From Abraham sprang the great tribes of Judaism, Christianity and Islam. From Abraham we learned, all of us, what it means to hope against hope and to cling to your gracious promise no matter what.

Therefore we join together with choirs of angels . . .

Holy, holy, holy Lord . . .

Blessed are you O God, and blessed is our brother Jesus who, out of his absolute faith in your promise of life, turned his face toward the certain death awaiting him in Jerusalem and encouraged his disciples to do the same. 'Those who want to save their life will lose it, and those who lose their life for my sake, and for the sake of the gospel, will save it', he said. We praise you, our Father, that these words proved to be true, both for him and for everyone who places their faith in him. For by Christ's death, and by his resurrection and glorious ascension, we who were dead in our sins are indeed brought to life, snatched from the grip of the evil one, raised up to a future full of peace and joy in believing . . .

Lent

. . . It is truly right to praise you, O God, for you care for your people as a mother cares for her young. Without price or bill of sale, you invite us to your table of plenty. You feed us with good food. You satiate our thirst. We praise you God because, even when we turn from your care and wander out into dry and weary lands, you do not abandon us. When we conjur seed from nothingness to to replace your own, and when the fruit we eat turns to dust in our mouths, even then we remain in your heart. You send your prophets to call us back, back to your table of plentiful love. 'Come again,' you say. 'Come drink the water that will quench your thirst for evermore.'

Therefore, with angels and saints . . .

Holy, holy, holy Lord . . .

You are holy, O God of grace, and blessed is your Son, Jesus Christ, whom you sent to share our hunger and husband our fruitfulness. When your people become dry and lifeless like figs that wither on the tree, Jesus appeared to inspire us once more. By the words of his mouth and the care of his hands, he breathed life into our fragile frames. By his death and his resurrection, he turned the seed that was dead into fruit so abundant that it spills out from the vessels that would contain it, increasing hundredfold on hunderedfold, enough to feed the whole hungry world . . .

Lent

. . . It is truly right to praise you, O God, for from the beginning you have been the light and hope for creation. By word and by light you breathed your vitality into Adam, and he became a living being. When your people were slaves in Egypt you sent Miriam and Moses to share the word that would light their path to freedom. When your people again turned from you, in sin and forgetfulness, you spoke up again in prophet, sage and stranger, fiercely fighting for your people's future

Most of all we praise you, God, for sending your Son, Jesus. When all the prophets were dead, and oppression reigned once more, he looked upon the city and wept for its sin. Though the sin of that city eventually killed him, we praise you, God, for raising your Son and, by his grace, gathering all your scattered children into the shelter of your household.

Therefore, with angels and saints . . .

Holy, holy, holy Lord . . .

You are holy, O God of glory, and holy is the face of your Son, Jesus Christ. In him your word and your breath have come to dwell with us, light for the world and hope for your people Israel . . .

Easter

. . . It is truly right and our greatest joy to give you praise, most Holy God, because in Christ Jesus you looked upon your lost and despairing people with mercy. Heeding our cry for help, you lifted your people out of death's dark depths and poured out your healing and forgiveness with generous liberality. While weeping may have overcome us for a long and bitter night, rejoicing came with the resurrection dawn. By the empty tomb you turned your people's wailing into dancing. You removed our bitter disgrace and clothed us with the joy of the baptised. For in Christ we died, in Christ we were buried, and in Christ we rose to live forever in newness of life.

Therefore, with angels and saints . . .

Holy, holy, holy Lord . . .

You are holy O God of majesty, and blessed is your most holy Son, Jesus Christ our Lord. Walking with us the path of grief, he opened our eyes to the joyful promises of Scripture. Sharing with us the bread and the wine of salvation, he set our hearts on fire with a passion to share the good news of your love with everyone we meet . . .

Easter

. . . Blessed are you, O God, and worthy of praise for ever and ever. At the beginning of the universe, when everything was dark and chaos reigned, you said 'let there be light!' and there was. By your word and your Spirit what was dead and nothing became alive and took form. And it was good.

When your people were languishing in Egypt under the dead weight of an evil despot, you sent forth Moses and Miriam. By their obedience you said to Pharoh 'let my people go!' And he did. Through the desert and through the water you led your people to life in the land of promise.

When his disciples had scattered, and the few who remained clung to each other in fear, your Son Jesus rose from his tomb and stood amongst them saying 'peace be with you!' By his life, his death and his resurrection, you took the dead bones of their broken faith and raised them to life.

Therefore, with angels and saints . . .

Easter

. . . It is truly right and our greatest joy to give you praise, most Holy God, for by the resurrection of your son from the dead you have made all things new, things in heaven and things on earth. Now your dwelling-place is forever with us, this fragile flesh, this faithless humanity. Because you love us you have thrown your lot in with us forever. In Christ, you are irrevocably *our* God and we are always and forever *your* people. Christ came singing a song of redemption. What you intended he accomplished. Now all who cry out in grief or pain may look forward to a future bright with hope, when every tear will be wiped away and every broken heart comforted.

Therefore, with angels and saints . . .

Holy, holy, holy Lord . . .

You are holy O God of majesty, and blessed is your most holy Son, Jesus Christ our Lord. On the cross where he died, on this hated symbol of our failure and shame, you opened a portal to a new universe, a world may new in the brightness of your glory. In him, our ruin and our new beginning, you have poured out the water of eternal life, that all who are thirsty might drink and so live with you for ever . . .

Trinity

. . . It is truly right to praise you, O God, for in the beginning your Spirit brooded over the chaos and brought forth life. By your Word you raised land from the oceans and creatures from the dust. In your image you made humankind, and gave us the stewardship of all you had made. We bless you God because even when we turned aside from your Wisdom and wandered in darklands of sin and greed, you did not abandon us to our choices. You sent Moses and Miriam, and all the prophets, to woo us back to yourself. Finally, at the darkest of hours, you sent your Son, Jesus Christ. In him we saw and heard your Wisdom in a human face, a Wisdom strong enough to conquer even sin and death. We bless you, God because, in him, you raised your broken people to a joyful communion with you in the dance of your lovingkindness.

Therefore, with the angels and saints . . .

Holy, holy, holy Lord . . .

You are holy, O Father of glory, and holy is your Son Jesus Christ. When he departed to be with you, he yet came to us anew in the companionship of the Holy Spirit. And you came too, to make us your church, the suffering body of your Son and the womb from which your reign of peace is born afresh . . .

Ordinary Time

. . . We bless you, O God, for you are the creator, the maker of heaven and earth. In ancient times you led your people through the barren desert to a fertile land full of fruit and rich produce. But, having arrived, your people defiled your gift and forgot about you entirely. The priests no longer enquired of you, and your just laws lay forgotten whilst the people pursued their worship of idols. You sent your prophets to call them back to your ways. But they were killed and imprisoned as troublemakers and traitors. In time you sent your own dear Son to us. In him we saw both your glory and your compassion. By his life and teaching, his death, and his resurrection to your side, he stirred our broken spirits to life once more.

Therefore, with the angels and saints . . .

Ordinary Time

. . . We bless you, O God, for you are the creator, the maker of heaven and earth. In the time of dreaming you fashioned a people for yourself from the clay of the earth. You gave them a land, your love, and everything that they needed. But they lusted for what is evil and marred themselves in the potter's hands. Not even your servants the prophets could call them back from the darkness into which they had descended.

In the fullness of time you sent Christ, your only son. He showed us what a well-made pot could look like. Living his life for others, he showed us how to love. Telling the truth, he showed us how to put aside deceit. Of course, he gained few fans in all this. The powers of his age put him to death on a cross. But praise be to you, Father of lights, by the Spirit you raised him from death as a sign that evil will not triumph.

Therefore, with the angels and saints . . .

Ordinary Time

. . . It is truly right and our greatest joy to give you praise, Holy God. You took our ancestors in faith from their slavery in Egypt, through the red sea and into the desert. There, at the Holy Mountain, you revealed yourself to them as a covenant-maker, one who sticks with us through thick and thin no matter what may come. As you found Elijah, your prophet, in despair in the desert – and gave him food and gently encouraged him after his many ordeals – so you find all your people at the point of their greatest need. When legions of devils have overcome us, you send your Son Jesus Christ to cast them out by the power of his love for us, and by his victory over death.

Therefore, with angels and saints . . .

Holy, holy, holy Lord . . .

You are holy O God of majesty, and blessed is your most holy Son, Jesus Christ our Lord. By our baptism into his death, you made all of us your children . . .

Ordinary Time

. . . We bless you, O God, for you are the creator, the maker of heaven and earth. We praise you God, for you are the one who breaks the drought with flooding rains, who causes the crops to multiply after many years of hunger, who fills the vats with oil and wine when joy and laughter seem but distant memories. You are the one who lovingly repays your people for the years the locust has eaten, for you are our God and there is no other. You are the one who pours out your Spirit on valleys of dry bones. You are the one who gives life to the dead and vision to those without sight. You are the one who is gracious to save everyone who calls on you, from the least to the greatest, whoever looks to you for mercy and help in their time of distress.

Therefore, with the angels and saints . . .

Holy, holy, holy Lord . . .

Blessed are you, O God, and blessed is your son, Jesus Christ. When the times were darkest of all, you sent him amongst us as light and life for all who despaired. By his life and teaching, by his humility on the cross, and by his exaltation to life in all its fullness, you taught us to worship you once more, and give our lives forever into your keeping . . .

All Saints or All Souls

. . . It is indeed right to give you our thanks and praise, O God, for through your prophet you promised a feast of rich food for all people, a banquet of aged wine and sweet meats to celebrate the passing of death into oblivion. For in Jesus Christ, through his death and resurrection, you came to swallow death up forever. In him, the stone is rolled away from our tombs, every tear is wiped away and the disgrace of your sinful people is removed forever. Christ is our resurrection and our life. Through the gift of his death, the tomb becomes a womb and we are born again.

And so, with angels and saints . . .

All Saints or All Souls

. . . We bless you, O God, for you are the creator, the maker of heaven and earth. You take pleasure in the people you have made and called to yourself. You adorn them with joy and with victory over evil. You mark us out with the seal of the Holy Spirit. You reveal to us your purpose from of old, to make everything alive in the Christ who is risen from the dead.

Therefore, with angels and saints . . .

Holy, holy, holy Lord . . .

Blessed are you, O God, and blessed is your son, Jesus Christ. You have put all things under his feet and made him the head of the church, which is his body. In him, the humble are exalted and the poor are made rich. In him the hungry are filled and the persecuted filled with joy eternal.

Reign of Christ

. . . We bless you, O God, for you are our Sovereign. Long ago you made covenant with Abraham and his kin, that you may be their God and they your people. In love you gave them a new land and granted them peace with their enemies. When they were enslaved in Egypt, you sent Moses to call them back to their homeland. By him, you gave them the law of life, a sign and a guide forever written in stone.

We bless you especially, God, because even when your people demanded another king, a frail king of flesh and blood, you did not turn your back on them. Through many dark years of sin and exile, when the Shepherds of Israel abandoned your ways, you remained faithful to your promises. Through the prophet you spoke of a new Shepherd, a king of flesh and blood, who would reign as you reign and love as you love.

Most of all, God our Sovereign, we praise you for that king's arrival in Jesus your son. From his cruciform throne we witnessed the staggering power of your loving-kindness. In him we learned that neither life, nor death, nor sin, nor all the powers of hell, could separate your people from their faithful Shepherd.

Therefore, with angels and saints . . .

Holy, holy, holy Lord . . .

Blessed are you, O God, and blessed is the king you sent to save us. Putting aside his authority, Jesus came amongst us as a servant and a slave. By his love, we who were lost are found. By his cross, we who were dead are made alive. By his resurrection, we who were nothing shall reign with Christ forever in his kingdom of peace . . .

EXHORATIONS OR LITANIES FOR THE SENDING OUT OF THE PEOPLE OF GOD

Advent

Lord, give us courage to prepare for your coming.

When we are tempted to busyness,

slow our bodies and still our hearts.
When we are tempted to enrich ourselves with *things*,
give us a longing for the riches of your kingdom.
When we are tempted to blow our savings
on people who lack for nothing,
give us hearts to serve the poor and the destitute.
When we are tempted to celebrate Christmas too early,
show us the joy of prayer and of waiting.

Lord, give us courage,
give us courage to wait for you in faith.

Christmas

Lord, we praise you for the gift of your Son.
Alleluia, alleluia!

In the fast-lane of work and family and saving the world,
slow our racing hearts, that we may recognise your gift.
Amidst the anxiety of providing for ourselves and our families,
slow our racing hearts, that we may recognise your gift.
When the greed of the mighty threatens to consume the whole world,
slow our racing hearts, that we may recognise your gift.
When the going gets tough, and we fear that joy has eluded us,
slow our racing hearts, that we may recognise your gift.

Lord, we praise you for the gift of your Son.
Alleluia, alleluia!

Lent

Let us affirm our Lenten covenant together:
When God's calls,
we shall listen.
Where God sends,
we shall go.
Where Christ goes before us,
we shall follow.

When the way becomes rough,
we shall call on the Spirit for courage.
When the way becomes dark,
we shall look to Christ for light.

When the way becomes lonely,
we shall lean on our kin.
When the way seems impossible,
we shall not give in,
for nothing is impossible for God.

Easter

The Lord says:
'People of St . . . . [name of congregation], do you love me?'
Yes, Lord, you know that we love you.
'Then show me that you mean it:
feed your children with the story of my love.'

'People of St . . . . , do you love me?'
Yes, Lord, you know that we love you.
'Then show me that you mean it:
care for the lost and the broken.'

'People of St . . . . , do you love me?'
Lord, you know everything; you know that we love you.
'Then show me that you mean it:
share your Easter faith with anyone who will listen.'

When you are young in faith, the world is your oyster. You believe that you can do whatever you choose. When you are grown up, you will recognise that freedom and glory come only to those who know how to submit themselves to God and his purposes. If you continue in my word, you are truly my disciples. You will know the truth, and the truth will set you free.

'People of St . . . . , take up your cross and follow me.'
Lord, you know that we love you.
We will follow you
all the way to the banqueting room of heaven.

Composed with Nathan Nettleton

Pentecost

As you go from this place, remember that you are children of God. The Spirit of Jesus bears witness, with your own spirits, that God is your Father. In God, everything worth having already belongs to you. You are the heirs of all God's most generous promises. So, go in faith.

Trust in God's call, and be prepared to go wherever the Spirit would take you. Be who you are called to be! You can, in the power of the Spirit!

Reconciliation Week

As you go,
remember that the Spirit whispers in your ear all the day long.
She whispers her message of love and liberation;
she beckons for you to follow her into paths as yet unimagined.
Go from this place as people of the Spirit,
people unafraid to dream and to vision,
to lament and to protest,
to work and to pray until the Kingdom is come.

Refugee Sunday

As you go from this place, remember that God has given you rest and refuge under the shelter of his wings. There, close to the Father's heart, you experience mercy, rejoicing, and peace that passes all understanding. Go now as God's ambassadors. How beautiful are the feet of those who bring the good news of God's safe haven to all the refugees of our world.

All Saints or All Souls

As you go from this place, remember God's high calling. In Christ you are ordained, set aside, to forsake the vain fashions of this world, and to set your heart and hope upon the new world that God is bringing into being. Seek justice, love mercy, and walk humbly with your God after the way of Christ. To this you have been called. In this is your glory, and the glory of all the saints.

Printed in the USA
CPSIA information can be obtained
at www.ICGtesting.com
LVHW091513170824
788411LV00004B/128

9 781923 206403